TODAY'S GLORY STORIES

FANNING THE FLAMES OF REVIVAL

Other books by Pamela Bolton:

Ushering in Revival and Awakening

God on the Move—Fanning the Flames of Revival

Circuit Riders—Fanning the Flames of Revival

Lady Preachers—Fanning the Flames of Revival

Today's Glory Stories

FANNING THE FLAMES OF REVIVAL

WRITTEN
AND
COMPILED
BY
PAMELA BOLTON

Today's Glory Stories
Fanning the Flames of Revival
by Pamela Bolton
Printed in the United States of America

1st Edition
ISBN: 978-1-7349220-2-8

http://www.pamelabolton.com
http://outoftheboxworshipcenter.com

TODAY'S GLORY STORIES

FANNING THE FLAMES OF REVIVAL

CONTENTS

DEDICATION ....
FOREWORD ....
INTRODUCTION ....

1. Telling Others How Great Our God Is 1
2. Phew! That Was A Close Call..7
3. God's Presence and Purpose 11
4. We Can Only Go This Far…...15
5. When the Fireworks Fizzle...19
6. In God's Hands...23
7. The Dream 25
8. The "Show & Tell" Gospel...29
9. Healing Comes in Many Forms....................................33
10. Angel on Assignment 39
11. From Intoxicated to Liberated!...................................43
12. God of The Impossible 49
13. Divine Encounter..53
14. Encounter with the Healer 59
15. God's Faithful Deliverance in The Midst of Evil 63

16. Secrets from the "Secret Place" 73
17. New Words in an Old House 77
18. Love Like This 81
19. Lovesick for You 89
20. Enjoying Intimacy with Our Lord 95
21. Math Lessons for Life 97
22. What Shall I Do? 101
23. Overcoming Faith 105

IN CLOSING 109
SALVATION PRAYER 111
ACKNOWLEDGEMENTS 113

Dedication

This book is also dedicated to you, dear reader.

Before you were formed in your mother's womb, God had a plan for your life. I want you to be encouraged to believe Him for all that He desires for your time on Earth… His plans for you are always good!

My heart's desire for you is this:

That you will have a real, living relationship with Jesus Christ, if you don't already.

That you will learn of Him.

That you will walk in His ways.

That you will be encouraged and empowered to be all that He wants you to be.

That you will know what His Word says about your life.

That you will believe that His Word is always true, regardless of what you see going on in the world around you.

That you will experience all that He has for you on this planet, including healing and provision of all your needs.

That you will continually be transformed into His image and likeness.

That you will fulfill your call on Earth.

"If you seek nothing but the will of God, He will always put you in the right place at the right time." –Smith Wigglesworth

FOREWORD

PASTOR CHARLIE MULLER

Victory Church, Albany and Colonie, New York

Pamela Bolton put together this incredible book to literally fan your flame for personal revival. Get ready to experience some insight into the miracle working power of God. The Bible instructs us to be still and know that He is God.

Today, as you take time to read this book, you will begin to see how the people who have been waiting on the Lord are the same people who display the very works of God. Waiting for God is not laziness; waiting for God is not effort. Waiting for God means "activity under command"! When you read this book, you will begin to understand what it means to walk by faith.

I would encourage every one of you to take the examples written herein and allow them to speak to you personally. The heart of the author is that each one of us will walk in the supernatural power of God.

This book speaks to the very core of my existence. In my personal life, I have experienced the power of God when I have prayed my way through, while waiting, acting, and receiving.

Enjoy the adventure you are about to experience, and may your life never be the same.

INTRODUCTION

One morning as I was waking up out of a sound sleep, it just came to me… the next book will be a devotional… a devotional about what God has done in the lives of ordinary people… how He has moved in power in their lives. Every believer has a story to tell, and their stories need to be told, especially in the day and hour in which we're living. We need to encourage one another with what God has done in the past so that we can believe Him for even greater things today.

The Word of God is filled with accounts of God's supernatural power at work in the lives of ordinary people… people just like you and me… people who were flawed… people who made mistakes… people who sometimes missed it… people who felt unworthy to be used by God. If you can relate to these kinds of people, you are a prime candidate to have God work powerfully in your life.

God wants us to walk in FAITH… to be settled in our hearts about what we believe and why we believe it… to take Him at His Word, all the time, even when we don't see anything happening in the natural realm. God's Word is always true! We have to get this fact settled in our hearts and minds.

God is still the God of miracles. He spoke everything into existence that we can see with the natural eye… everything! Nothing was created, except by the mouth of God. Jesus commissioned all believers to go and do what He had done… to represent Him on the planet… that includes each one of us living today. What an awesome responsibility was given in that moment when He spoke those words….

Would He give us a command that He would not empower us to fulfill? Surely He would not, so we need to go forth in the power of the Holy Spirit, believing for His perfect will to be fulfilled in our lives… believing that He wants us healed and whole in every area of our lives… believing that He will give us all that we need to do what He's called us to do on this planet… continually walking in faith… and being a doer of the Word of God.

"There are four principles we need to maintain: First, read the Word of God. Second, consume the Word of God until it consumes you. Third, believe the Word of God. Fourth, act on the Word." –Smith Wigglesworth

Part 1

Ordinary People Touched By An Extraordinary God

Day 1

Telling Others How Great Our God Is

However, Jesus did not permit him, but said to him, "Go home to your friends, and tell them what great things the Lord has done for you, and how He has had compassion on you." And he departed and began to proclaim in Decapolis all that Jesus had done for him; and all marveled. **Mark 5:19-20 (NKJV)**

I thought it good to declare the signs and wonders that the Most High God has worked for me. How great are His signs, And how mighty His wonders! His kingdom is an everlasting kingdom, And His dominion is from generation to generation. **Daniel 4:2-3 (NKJV)**

The second time I shared my story of dying and being in Heaven was in a United Methodist Church in Seattle, Washington. That day, I met an elderly lady who was 91 years old. I remember being guided to her by the pastor after the service. He told me that there was someone he wanted me to meet. She was sitting in a wheelchair at the back of the church sanctuary.

When I was finally standing next to her, I looked down at her wonderful face, straight into her eyes, and I knew she believed. To this day I will always remember what I saw. I could see great joy in her eyes, along with an appreciation for what she had just heard. Her eyes told me that she had faith. I had heard people talk about that kind of faith, but prior to this event, I had never seen it like that.

I believe Peter and John encountered that same look on the face of the crippled man whose story is told in Acts 3:1-10. In these verses, you can read about this man who was brought to beg at the same temple gate every day. Most likely, he had heard of all the marvelous miracles that had been done by Peter and John in the name of Jesus.

The following verses tell what the lame man was exposed to:

Then fear came upon every soul, and many wonders and signs were done through the apostles.
Acts 2:43 (NKJV)

So continuing daily with one accord in the temple, and breaking bread from house to house, they ate their food with gladness and simplicity of heart, praising God and having favor with all the people. And the Lord added to the church daily those who were being saved.
Acts 2:46-47 (NKJV)

And a certain man lame from his mother's womb was carried, whom they laid daily at the gate of the temple which is called Beautiful, to ask alms from those who entered the temple; **Acts 3:2 (NKJV)**

So, when they looked into his eyes, there was faith that was exchanged; and the man was healed.

...who, seeing Peter and John about to go into the temple, asked for alms. And fixing his eyes on him, with John, Peter said, "Look at us." So he gave them his attention, expecting to receive something from them. Then Peter said, "Silver and gold I do not have, but what I do have I give you: In the name of Jesus Christ of Nazareth, rise up and walk." And he took him by the right hand and lifted him up, and immediately his feet

and ankle bones received strength. So he, leaping up, stood and walked and entered the temple with them—walking, leaping, and praising God. And all the people saw him walking and praising God. Then they knew that it was he who sat begging alms at the Beautiful Gate of the temple; and they were filled with wonder and amazement at what had happened to him.
Acts 3:3-10 (NKJV)

So, there I was looking into this 91-year-old woman's eyes, and what did I see? FAITH! What followed was an amazing exchange. It seemed like her eyes were saying, "Thank you, thank you, thank you." Then, they seemed to change a little, and I perceived that she was saying, "Will you come and visit me?"

I spoke aloud to her, "I will come and see you."

She then lifted her arm and gently took ahold of the front of my shirt below my chin. She slowly pulled me down and spoke in my ear, "When?"

Softly, I responded, "Soon."

Others around me rejoiced and cried for joy. When I looked at the pastor, he had a big smile on his face. I thought that they were happy because my wife, Marilyn, and I were going to visit this lady sometime in the near future.

Later that day, the pastor told me that the lady had a stroke a few weeks before we came, and she could not talk or move. So, when she pulled me down and asked, "When?" that was the first word she had spoken since having the stroke. Her pulling me down with her arm and hand was the first time she moved any part of her body without help.

I was not aware that God had just healed her. At the time, I assumed she was just happy to hear my story about dying and going to Heaven. I did not know that this testimony about God in my life could heal a person physically.

Marilyn and I did go see her a few weeks later in a nursing home. When we got there, we were escorted to a visiting room. A few minutes later, the 91-year-old lady walked into the room without assistance. She was followed by her daughter. We talked to her for about an hour and a half. Her daughter sat in on the visit and shed tears of joy. They both gave us big hugs and let us know she was being released to go home in few days. She had only been living there because of the stroke, but now she was healed by Jesus and could go back home. You should have seen the smile on her face! They both thanked us so much for coming and for the healing that took place. We thanked them both and said, "That is Jesus!"

Since that time, I have seen faith build in people when I have shared my story about **How Great Our God Is**, and over the years, many have been healed both physically and emotionally while listening to it. I believe each of us who are "born again" have faith building stories to tell about our God… the stories about what Jesus has done in our lives that can help others build their faith to the point of physical and/or emotional healing. So, I encourage you to remember what God has done and is doing for you. Take your story and tell others about how great your God is, and watch their faith be built up so that they, too, can be healed.

PRAYER

Father,

I thank you for the many miracles You have done in my life. Help me now to share them with others so they can have their faith built up. As their faith grows in You, heal them physically and emotionally. Thank you, Father.

In Jesus' Name, Amen.

And they overcame him by the blood of the Lamb and by the word of their testimony, and they did not love their lives to the death. **Revelation 12:11 (NKJV)**

Dean Braxton*, Author of In Heaven*
Ashburn, Virginia

DAY 2

PHEW! THAT WAS A CLOSE CALL

For He will save you from the trap of the fowler, And from the deadly pestilence. **Psalm 91:3 (AMP)**

"Phew! THAT was a close call." Have you ever uttered those five words as you let out a deep breath of relief after a dangerous incident? If so, then you, too, just may have experienced God's ***supernatural protection***.

One evening, a couple of months ago, I was on my way home, driving down a sparsely lit country road. It had been such a long day, and I was so looking forward to getting home, getting comfy, and getting in my bed. There was music playing on my car stereo and various thoughts playing on my mind as I cruise controlled my way down this familiar route. As I navigated around a sharp bend, suddenly a very large deer bounded from the right side of the road and directly in front of my car. In a flash, my eyes scanned my surroundings, and I realized that there was nowhere for me to go to avoid this "accident." There was a steel road barrier on the right side of the road preventing me from pulling off to the side, oncoming traffic going 55 mph on the left, and cars following a close distance behind me preventing me from slamming on the brakes. Mentally out of options in this split second of thought, I simply braced for impact with the deer... but a miracle happened. We never collided. Somehow the deer had made it to the other side of the road without being hit by my car or any others. Despite everything happening so quickly, I realized that when both my surroundings and my reaction time would have failed me, God had supernaturally protected me from what surely would have been a terrible collision.

Ironically, the next evening, I was heading home at around the same time, driving towards the same exact place that I'd almost had the incident with the deer. I was vigilant this time, peering into the darkness on the sides of the road for any rogue deer that may try to dash in front of my car. Fortunately, there were no deer, but as I rounded the same sharp bend, all of a sudden, a huge 18-wheeler truck began crossing from the left side of the road directly into my lane! Again, the steel road barrier was on the right side blocking me from pulling off of the road, and the truck came into my lane so quickly that I had no time to react and again just braced for impact... but it didn't happen. It was yet another miracle! I am convinced that God, again, supernaturally protected me. Moments later when I looked into my side view mirror, I could still see that same truck behind me, fully in my lane!

While I suspect that the driver of the truck may have fallen asleep and crossed lanes, I know that I serve a God who neither slumbers nor sleeps ("Behold, He that keepeth Israel shall neither slumber nor sleep" Psalm 121:4, KJV). The God we serve is always vigilant in His protection of us! In this world, there are many dangers that we know to avoid, but God provides His promise of protection for us even when it comes to the hidden attacks that the enemy tries to send our way, when we least expect them!

Psalm 91 is my go-to scripture to pray over my family and myself for daily protection, but the verse that I cling to in events like these is Psalm 91:3. I like the way that the Good News Translation emphasizes that He will keep you safe from ALL traps of the enemy and from ALL deadly pestilences. Not a couple, not some, not even most, but ALL. We can hold onto this promise from God and be confident that even in the midst of a pandemic, or after a negative report on the news or from the doctor's office, or any other danger that may come our way unexpectedly, we can trust that our God has good plans for our lives and that He will keep us safe.

I pray God gives you a fresh revelation of His supernatural protection in your life and the lives of those you love today… that you include this scripture in your prayers to Him and confidently believe that if He says it, He will do it!

For He will save you from the trap of the fowler, And from the deadly pestilence. **Psalm 91:3 (AMP)**

N. Wilson*, Outreach Coordinator*
Out of the Box Worship Center
Whitehall, New York

DAY 3

GOD'S PRESENCE AND PURPOSE

MY OUT-OF-BODY EXPERIENCE

"And whoever lives and believes in Me shall never die."
–Jesus Christ, John 11:26 (NKJV)

My faith has always guided me throughout my life. As a young girl, I would go with my Grandmother Pond to her Thursday night Bible studies. I grew up in a Christian family, and I sang in our church choir for over 70 years.

I have had three severe anaphylactic reactions in my life, and the third one brought on my near-death experience.

One evening, as I was taking clothes off the line, a honeybee stung me. Right away, I gave myself an Epinephrine injection. As I started to feel the tingling in my nose and face, I knew that it wasn't going to be good. My throat started to swell, and it was hard for me to breath.

It was a four-mile trip to my doctor's office. Upon arrival, I was unconscious and unresponsive. As I laid upon the exam table, I found myself looking down at my body and watching Dr. Michael Lynch try to save my life. I heard him say, "I don't know if I can save her or not."

It was then that I saw the lighted path of peace and warmth. As Acts 9:3 says, "...and suddenly a light shone around him from heaven (NKJV)." Jesus was in a white robe on a mountain, and He said to me, "Go back, for I have much for you to do." Matthew 17:2 says, "His face shone like the sun, and His clothes became as white as the light (NKJV)." That's how He looked.

As my body came back to life, a warm feeling filled me as I started to focus on those around me. I could feel the swelling in my face and arms, and I was covered with big red blotches. The rescue squad was there to take me to the hospital to stay overnight.

It wasn't until a month later when I saw Dr. Lynch and was telling him of my experience–that I had seen and heard him talking–that He told me I had had an out-of-body experience. I had never heard of this before.

For a while, I kept quiet about this humbling experience. For who would believe me? But as I grew in my faith, I knew that I was supposed to witness. John 11:26 says, "And whoever lives and believes in Me shall never die (NKJV)."

You are never the same person physically or spiritually after a life and death experience. Psalm 36:9 says, "For with You is the fountain of life, In Your light we see light (NKJV)." God showed me my purpose and priority in life is to help others. Now, I have confidence in knowing that He is always with me and guiding me to fulfill His job.

God whispers to us through the Holy Spirit; and I've learned over the years to listen to His still, small voice.

Back in March of 1972, I really learned the importance of listening to the Holy Spirit. My 3-year-old son, Douglas, disappeared in the woods; and we were out looking for him. I had left an area, but I kept having a nagging feeling to go back there. Then, I heard that still, small voice say to me, "Go back, go back." I went back, and there was my son, floating in a pond. He had turned blue. A stranger who was at the farm pulled him out of the cold water and revived him. If I hadn't listened to the voice of God, my son wouldn't be alive today.

Each day, I walk with hope and strength knowing that God is always with me. Each morning, I ask Him, "What would You like me to do today, and whom may I touch with your love?"

My intimate communication with Him brings me peace and joy in spite of life's tribulations. I am always aware that the Holy Spirit is with me, and I am always aware of His presence.

God desires that you learn to recognize His voice, too. He is not a respecter of persons, and if He does something for one, He'll do it for others as well. His Word says that His sheep know His voice. Be blessed as you grow in your relationship with Jesus and learn to communicate with Him on a daily basis.

Because of my near-death experience, God has guided me to do many things for my church, community, school, friends, and family. He still has much for me to do even after this experience that took place 45 years ago. Today, I move forward in life with faith and confidence, and I know that when God calls me home, Heaven is waiting with love and peace.

***Lila Myer**, Woman of God*
Granville, New York

Day 4

We Can Only Go This Far....

But Jesus looked at them and said to them, "With men this is impossible, but with God all things are possible." **Matthew 19:26 (NKJV)**

Have you lived long enough to have life's circumstances bring you to a place in your journey where you were forced to say, "I can only go this far...."? Other ways to say this would be: "This is as far as I can go...," or "I just can't go any further...." If you have not yet experienced a circumstance in life that would cause you to say this or feel this way, I give you this promise: You will!

As a matter of fact, in Matthew 5:45, Jesus said that life's circumstances are not respecters of persons. Speaking symbolically, He was saying that rain, storms, and contrary winds will come to all people at one time or another.

Job 14:1 tells us that if you are born from a woman (that means all living people), you can expect years of life accompanied with trouble.

In Matthew 19:26, when Jesus was speaking, with his words it seems that He was trying to capture our complete focus and let us know there are not only days of trouble from time to time awaiting us, but there are also significant circumstances we will face that glare with impossibility from our perspective.

The Bible offers many examples of people who felt like they could only go so far. Let me highlight two examples:

Moses and the Israelites were facing the impassable Red Sea. In other words, they felt, “We can only go this far….” In their minds, this became a place of impossibility. The servant of Elisha saw the enemy’s army surrounding them and felt trapped as if to say, “We can only go this far….” To the servant, this became a place of impossibility.

Jesus confirmed that there will be situations that will be impossible for you and me to deal with. However, continuing to look at the words of Jesus, He didn’t leave us in the so-called place of impossibility. He did not leave us stranded, feeling hopeless. In Matthew 19:26, He said, “With men this is impossible, but with God all things are possible (KJV).

When we read these words, “with God all things are possible,” they cause hope to leap into our hearts. I encourage you to look at the idea of, “We can only go this far…,” not as a point of limitation but as the point where God goes where we cannot go and does what we cannot do. It is not a place of limitation; it is a breeding ground for God’s miracles to take place in our lives.

Moses and the Israelites watched as God created a highway in the sea so that they could cross on dry ground, and Elisha prayed for his servant’s eyes to be opened so he could see the host of heavenly chariots surrounding the enemy’s army.

Watching God go where we cannot go and do what we cannot do changes my outlook on the phrase, “We can only go this far!”

Please allow me to tell you why this devotion means so much to me….

Sixty-five years ago, on the 19th of November, my mother gave birth to me, only to be told by her doctor that I would not live through the night. I had a hole in my heart, and surgery was not available at that time; but my parents knew of another answer, "Jesus the Healer!" So, they made their way down the hall to where they found me in an incubator with blue skin, gasping for air. They put their hands on the window that separated us, and they said, "Jesus, **We Can Only Go This Far….** We ask You to go the rest of the way. Touch him and heal him." As of this writing, 65 years later, I testify that Jesus is still the Healer! He did what He does best. He goes where we cannot go and does what we cannot do, because "We can only go this far!" Praise the Lord!

The next time you feel you can only go so far, remember at that very moment and place, you are standing on God's breeding ground for your needed miracle. Open your heart and receive it.

LET'S PRAY….

Dear Jesus,

Thank You for Your revelation that when we feel we can only go so far, that is when You go where we cannot go and do what we cannot do. Because of this truth, I will walk and follow the steps You have ordered for me, never worrying again knowing, "I can only go this far."

Amen

***Reverend Lamar Cooper**, Revivalist*
Miamisburg Assembly of God
Miamisburg, Ohio

DAY 5

WHEN THE FIREWORKS FIZZLE

***"Therefore I say to you, whatever things you ask when you pray, believe that you receive them, and you will have them."* Mark 11:24 (NKJV)**

As Christians, we are called to "walk by faith, not by sight," 2 Corinthians 5:7 (NKJV). Yet, it seems we are so quick to lose heart when we pray for things and don't see them manifest. I have been guilty of this; I will be so full of faith and pray a fiery prayer for healing. "In the name of Jesus Christ," I ask, I plead, I command, I decree and... nothing seems to happen. One time, I prayed such a prayer; and it shifted my theology.

A colleague of mine at a private Christian school had possibly sprained her ankle the previous day, and it was swollen to twice its normal size. She limped around the halls all day getting everyone's personal diagnosis and advice. Someone even offered to bring in crutches.

At the end of the day, I walked into our after-school meeting. It had been a very trying day for me, and I was tired and dispirited. I saw her sitting there at a table, the first one in the room. I looked down at her swollen foot, conflicted. I asked if anyone had prayed for her, and we were both astounded to realize that no one had.

Not one soul, all day long, in a Christian school, in a *pentecostal church*, had offered to pray for her. Why? Was the resulting miracle too much to ask for? Unrealistic? Praying for a headache was one thing, but for a visibly damaged limb? Daunting for sure, I get it… hence, my internal conflict. But my obedience won out. I got down on my knees and prayed the worst stumbling, mumbling prayer of my life. To make it worse, as I crouched there with my hand on her foot, another teacher came in and began chatting away, clearly unaware that I was calling on the throne room of God for a miracle here. Needless to say, the atmosphere was anything but "spiritual." There were no warm "tinglies," no background piano music, no angels, no lightning, no nothing. I said, "Amen," and I got up.

Later that night, I sat in my truck rolling the event around in my head, analyzing the different angles. Nothing had happened; so, did that mean I was to blame? I certainly couldn't blame GOD! Maybe I had done it wrong... not asked the Holy Spirit to come... not laid hands properly or fasted enough... but I had to be objective, not critical. None of my hypotheses were scriptural. I had used the name of Jesus Christ in faith just like the Bible teaches. When it all boils down, the only thing that mattered was the name of Jesus. Regardless of the result, I knew that my *experience* didn't change the *truth* of scripture.

I immediately felt peace in my heart and a vibration in my pocket. It was Facebook notifying me that I had been tagged in a post: My friend had left school in a lot of pain, but as soon as she got home and stepped out of her minivan, she received instant and miraculous healing!

Who knows why she wasn't healed the moment I prayed, but Jesus was always teaching His disciples and coaching them, not doing everything for them and not making sure they never made mistakes? There was always space for questions. Many times, things happened in ways that the disciples did not expect, but Jesus always knew what He was doing. It wasn't always just about the miracle, but about the message or the lesson.

The next day at work, we all saw the undeniable evidence of God's goodness. It truly was a miracle. God received the glory, and many of us were humbled and inspired.

More than once, something like this has happened, where I have prayed a healing prayer in faith and seen nothing happen outwardly; but then later (sometimes years later), I have heard the testimony of the power of those prayers or seen their fruit.

Fruit takes time to grow. Sometimes miracles do too. Sometimes miracles are happening, but they aren't always "textbook," happening the way we might expect them to. Jesus hardly ever did the same miracle twice in the same way.

We are to study THE BOOK–THE BIBLE–and to follow its teachings, but we should never forget that Jesus Himself is THE WORD. His testimony is still being written. We are to be operating out of relationship with God, obedience to Him, and love for broken humanity. There is no formula for this—but Jesus!

He wants you to come to Him each time, in each new situation, to receive *living* water; *fresh* revelation. He doesn't have a well full of stale, prefab miracles to draw from. His mercies are *new* each day. Each prayer we offer is an act of love and a leap of faith. We cannot please God without faith, and we cannot make a difference without love. More often than not, love is the biggest sign and wonder.

Above all else, regardless of whether or not a miracle happens, know that you have been given the greatest thing you can ever receive, which is Jesus.

"...But if You can do anything, have compassion on us and help us."

Jesus said to him, "If you can believe, all things are possible to him who believes."

Immediately the father of the child cried out and said with tears, "Lord, I believe; help my unbelief!"
Mark 9:22-24 (NKJV)

"Therefore I say to you, whatever things you ask when you pray, believe that you receive them, and you will have them." **Mark 11:24 (NKJV)**

***Nicole Banta**, Missionary*
Granville, New York

Day 6

In God's Hands

For He shall give His angels charge over you, to keep you in all your ways. In their hands they shall bear you up, lest you dash your foot against a stone.
Psalm 91:11-12 (NKJV)

It was midday in November, right after lunch, and it was a decent day as far as the weather was concerned. We, a crew of men that included three others and me, were working in an area that was flat but on a hill. We had been clearing an area of trees and brush for the local power company.

When I was walking over to pick up some brush, I tripped on a stump and went head first over a thirty-five-foot cliff. I landed face down on the ground beside some railroad tracks, which were on some large rocks. I was in a mudhole. I got up, and with the help of the crew, I got back up the cliff by rope.

I was driven to the hospital by my boss. The hospital did CT scans, and I was told that everything looked good. The only problems that I had were a fractured hand and my front teeth had been knocked out.

My boss at the time said that day had changed him, because he knew that I was going to be dead when he looked over the cliff, but I actually went back to work the next day.

Today, I give God all the glory because I should have been hurt much worse or even killed. I know that my life is in God's hands but not only my life… Be encouraged today, because your life is in His hands as well.

***Jeff Hatfield**, Pastor*
Crane Creek Pentecostal Holiness Church
Crane Creek, West Virginia

Day 7

The Dream

***And it shall come to pass afterward, that I will pour out My Spirit on all flesh; your sons and your daughters shall prophesy, your old men shall dream dreams, your young men shall see visions.* Joel 2:28 (KJV)**

It's true that God works in mysterious ways. All my Christian life, I had read about and heard about prophetic dreams. I was a "pizza dreamer," if you know what I mean. Any dreams I had were probably the result of pizza before bedtime. Beyond that, I rarely remembered my dreams, at least in their entirety. I might remember a few of the things that happened in a dream, but that was it.

This time was different! The local Baptist Church in town was in the middle of a transition that had begun when they decided they could no longer support the old brick church they had occupied since the 1950s. The few remaining congregants were part of the board that made decisions about the facility, and they had let it be known that their prayerful desire was that the church be sold to a ministerial group, preferably a church that would continue to use it for the Lord's work. They had put out the word that any ministry desiring to take over the facility should write a letter of intent saying what they would do with the church building should they be chosen. Around six or eight ministries, including the local Baptist group in Bennington and us, showed interest and submitted letters.

Now, on to my dream… I went to bed that night, not having the church building on my mind and fell asleep rather quickly. Suddenly, in the dream, the voice of the Lord came to me. Don't ask me how I knew it was God, I just did. He said,

"Timmy (my parents called me that), I want you to listen to me."

I said, "OK, Lord."

He continued, "The church is going to be given to the Baptist group."

I said, "OK."

He said, "I want you to remember this dream."

I said, "I will."

He said again, rather emphatically, "I said, remember the dream." I guess He knew I rarely did. He continued, "They will quickly turn it down."

I said, "Alright."

"Then I want you to 'move forward'," He said. I thought that was a strange choice of words. He didn't say, "Take the church" or "occupy the church." He said "I want you to 'move forward'." I said that I would. Then after warning me again to remember the dream, He was gone.

Well, that was a weird dream, but I remembered it well and told my wife and only a few others about it. Not too many days later, the lady from the Baptist Church Board called and told me the vote had been to give the church to the Baptist group. I told her if that was the Lord's will, that was fine. She said, "Well, I don't know if that's the Lord's will, but that's how they voted." I thanked her, and we hung up.

Only a few days went by, and she called again. I was standing near my wife when the phone rang, and I immediately said, "Here we go." She told me the Baptist Church group had turned it down and decided that now that was not the direction they were going to take. I said, "OK, so now what?"

She said, "I want to know if you want to 'move forward'." There it was… the same wording the Lord had used.

I immediately said, "Yes," fully believing God was at work; and after she told me that they would vote again, I made a request. I told her my dream and asked her, "Please don't mention this to anyone before they vote."

She asked me, "Why not?" and I told her that I didn't want to sway the vote… just let God's will be done. They voted unanimously to give the church to our ministry. Praise God!

After that, we wondered how we would maintain, let alone repair, such a large facility. Within a few short months, we received a bequest for over a half a million dollars. We did major renovations, and we give God all the glory! So now, I'm more than just a "pizza dreamer"! Thank you, Jesus!

Reverend Timothy Bohley*, Founder and Pastor*
Living Waters Evangelistic Ministries and Jacob's Well Fellowship
Cambridge, New York

Day 8

The "Show & Tell" Gospel

***For I will not dare to speak of any of those things which Christ has not accomplished through me, in word and deed, to make the Gentiles obedient—in mighty signs and wonders, by the power of the Spirit of God, so that from Jerusalem and round about to Illyricum I have fully preached the gospel of Christ.* Romans 15:18-19 (NKJV)**

For a period of time in my life, I would go to a local soup kitchen to pray and minister to people on a weekly basis. Sometimes my heart would break as I saw them come into this dark, dreary room to get a meal with their families. The food, although adequate, was not especially nutritious. They often ate in silence, and many had little joy in their hearts.

On one of those days at the soup kitchen, I walked in and saw a man sitting by himself, desperately trying to get the spoon to his mouth. Every move he made was accompanied by jerking motions. He was slowly able to feed himself. I felt such deep compassion for him. I went over, sat across from him, and asked, "May I pray for you when you are done eating?"

He gratefully answered, "I-I-I would a-a-a-ppreciate that." He struggled to get every word out, because his voice was shaking so badly.

I inquired, "What's wrong?"

He answered, "I have a neurological disease." He told me the name of the disease, but I had never heard of it before. Not wanting to embarrass him, I went and sat at another table until he was done eating.

As he got up from the table, I noticed that he was also walking with a slow, jerky gait. I directed him to a small chapel that was adjacent to the soup kitchen so that I could pray for him. I shared with him why Jesus would heal him, laid a hand on his shoulder, and began to ask God to touch him. All the while, he was shaking and jerking under my hand.

I prayed, "Lord, drive this all out. In Jesus' name, I command this disease to go from him." Right under my hand, all the shaking stopped. A look of total peace settled on him. It was beautiful and amazing to see the healing power of our God.

He looked at me with huge eyes and said, "I felt electricity go all through my body!" Then, with a now completely clear voice, this man cried out, "Lord, forgive me. I'm sorry. I have been so far from You. I give my life to You." Without a word from me, he called on the name of the Lord for salvation. As he walked away from me that day, the jerking and the shaking were gone. More than that, he walked out from there as a brand-new creation in Christ!

This man already knew he needed to repent, but my words alone would have been unlikely to produce genuine repentance. He needed to experience the goodness and the power of an Almighty God.

All forms of evangelism are valuable, but Paul speaks of how he fully preached the gospel through miracles. Miracles demonstrate the Risen Christ, and in fact, miracles are a part of the full gospel. The "Show and Tell" Gospel is God's master plan.

Healing the sick is not only for a select few. The Word does not say that apostles, prophets, evangelists, pastors, and teachers shall lay hands on the sick, and they will recover. If you are a believer, you qualify (Mark 16:18). In fact, the Word shows that every person that God sent out to preach the gospel, He also sent out to heal the sick. We are all commanded to "Go into all the world, and preach the gospel… (Mark 16:15, NKJV)."

This is good news! You are not lacking in any way. The power of God dwells inside of you through the person of the Holy Spirit. Allow the compassion of Jesus to fill your heart for this hurting world, and then, go for it. Last of all, never, never quit!

Reverend Sherry Evans, *Pastor and Author of Everyday Miracles*
Covenant Church
Jefferson, Ohio

DAY 9

HEALING COMES IN MANY FORMS

And His name* (Jesus), *through faith in His name, has made this man strong, whom you see and know. Yes, the faith which comes through Him has given him this perfect soundness in the presence of you all.
Acts 3:16 (NKJV)

I remember my mother telling me that when I was born, I was very sick; I was diagnosed with "Bacterial Meningitis." What is Bacterial Meningitis and how may it affect a person's life? According to *Web*MD, it is defined as: "a rare infection that affects the delicate membranes–called meninges–that cover the brain and spinal cord."

This infection affected me greatly when I was a baby. According to my mother, she was informed by the doctor that I would never be able to walk or run normally like other kids. He also said that I would have issues with remembering things due to brain damage.

My grandmother, God rest her saintly soul, would not take this negative news without a fight in prayer. I believe that she was a fairly new Christian at the time, but she believed that I could be healed in Jesus' name.

I vaguely remember when I was 3 years old, rolling around on the floor of our house in a walker. One day my stepfather, Jack, stated, "You're getting out of that walker and you are going to start walking."

This reminds me of the time when Jesus told the lame man at the pool to take up his mat and walk. John, Chapter 5, verses 2 through 9 speak of this encounter:

> ***Now there is in Jerusalem by the Sheep Gate a pool, which is called in Hebrew, Bethesda, having five porches. In these lay a great multitude of sick people, blind, lame, paralyzed, waiting for the moving of the water. For an angel went down at a certain time into the pool and stirred up the water; then whoever stepped in first, after the stirring of the water, was made well of whatever disease he had. Now a certain man was there who had an infirmity thirty-eight years. When Jesus saw him lying there, and knew that he already had been in that condition a long time, He said to him, "Do you want to be made well?"***
>
> ***The sick man answered Him, "Sir, I have no man to put me into the pool when the water is stirred up; but while I am coming, another steps down before me."***
>
> ***Jesus said to him, "Rise, take up your bed and walk." And immediately the man was made well, took up his bed, and walked.*** **(NKJV)**

That very same day, I started walking. The faith that my stepfather had was unquestionably undeniable. I trusted what he said, that I could start walking, and so I did. He proceeded to help me out of the walker, and I started walking all around the house. As I grew older, I started running around like other "normal" children.

I played a lot of football and basketball with the kids from the neighborhood, and when I was a sophomore, I started running around town a lot. One day, the school's track coach, Mr. Collier, saw me out running. As I was on my way to the playground, he pulled over and approached me. He asked me if I had ever considered trying out for track and field. The thought had never even occurred to me, because in my mind, my thoughts were always reverting back to what some doctors had said to my mother when I was born; I would never run competitively.

Running around town was one thing, but to compete as a track and field runner, that was an entirely different story. I decided to try it out.

I wasn't allowed to play football in high school for fear of breaking one or both of my legs; however, my step-father allowed me to join the track team. At first, it was very challenging due to the simple fact that I'd never trained for any track and field events before. Naturally, I felt intimidated.

Even running one or two-mile races was quite a feat for me, but my mother wouldn't let me quit. She made it to most of my competitions and would always cheer me on. She also told me to praise Jesus in my head while I ran, and that helped me out immensely. I often had the song "Awesome God" playing in my mind as I ran.

My grandmother would quote the Bible verse found in Colossians 3:23, which states, "And whatever you do, do it heartily, as to the Lord and not to men, (NKJV)." I used that as my inspiration.

My track coach was quite impressed with my ability to run long distance. He said that I had real potential, and he asked me to try out for cross country running in the fall. So, in my junior year of high school, I joined the cross-country team, but I had to learn some hard lessons during that time. I started getting cocky and not relying on the Lord as much, and I believe that He allowed certain things to happen to me to bring me back to Himself.

A couple of times, I sprained my ankles and twisted my knees, though I still didn't quit. I did exercises that would help me to get out on the track, so to speak. I placed my faith and trust in Jesus again and did really well in my senior year.

I was able to take 1st place in the 2-mile run in track and field at Sectionals. In cross country running, I almost made it to States on that final race. To God be the glory that I was able to do these things when I was pegged to fail in the beginning of my life. Today, I still have some of the awards that I won back then when I was a runner.

Nowadays, walking is the way to go for me since my job requires it. As an employee of the United States Postal Service, I'm required to deliver mail, mainly on foot, whether it's raining, snowing, or sleeting… as the saying goes. Finally, I always remind myself that I can do all things through Christ who strengthens me. Paul said to run the race and to finish it. I'm still running the race in a different sense, the Christian walk, racing to be with my Father in Heaven.

THERE IS POWER IN THE NAME OF JESUS

For there is no distinction between Jew and Greek, for the same Lord over all is rich to all who call upon Him. For "whoever calls on the name of the Lord shall be saved." **Romans 10:12-13 (NKJV)**

I can recall a time when I was in the Air Force when I invoked the name of Jesus to set myself free from oppression. It seems like it was just yesterday to me. I came home from church one evening after receiving a powerful message from the sermon that was given. I relaxed on my bed and turned the television on. I selected the Trinity Broadcasting Network for my viewing choice.

That night, I was watching people praise the Lord with familiar praise and worship songs. I joined in, closed my eyes, and praised along with them. I could feel God's presence very strongly in the room. This probably went on for about an hour or so. Then, I turned off the television and lay there drinking in the Holy Spirit. I prayed before I went to sleep as I always did, but I had a bit of trouble falling asleep, because I was so hyped up on the Holy Spirit.

All of a sudden, I felt like I couldn't move or speak. I was being weighed down by something that I had never encountered before. I was being silenced by something unseen, and I was unmovable. I laid there paralyzed and not knowing what was happening to me or why. I did start to panic, for like I said, I'd never had this happen to me before. I had to calm myself down and try to figure out how to get out of this predicament. It was then that I remembered the Bible verse that was preached to me over and over while I was growing up in church: "For 'whoever calls on the name of the LORD shall be saved' (Romans 10:13, NKJV)."

At first, I could only think of the name of Jesus in my mind. As soon as I thought of His name, this stronghold began to dissipate. I was then able to whisper the name of Jesus, and I began to have the ability to move. I still felt something on my chest that had a grip on me. Finally, I yelled the name of Jesus at the top of my lungs, and the evil spirit fled. I was set free!

Immediately, I got up and started praising God and thanking Jesus for what He had done for me. I praised Him for not only setting me free at that particular moment but for everything else He had done for me in my life as well. I felt peace that overcame my understanding, just like the Bible verse states in Philippians 4:7, "...and the peace of God, which surpasses all understanding, will guard your hearts and minds through Christ Jesus (NKJV)."

I thank God for the authority that we have over demons, devils, and evil spirits. We just need to always remember that we are the children of the Most High God. We were given authority over Satan through the name of Jesus. Just like the famous Christian song says, "There is power in the name of Jesus, to break every chain…." So, when you feel oppressed or depressed, call on the name of the Lord Jesus, and you too shall be saved!

***Lyle Hurlburt**, Christian Singer*
Out of the Box Worship Center
Whitehall, New York

Day 10

Angel on Assignment

For He shall give His angels charge over you, to keep you in all your ways. In their hands they shall bear you up, lest you dash your foot against a stone.
Psalm 91:11-12 (NKJV)

When I think back over my life, I can recall numerous times that God preserved my family and me. One of the incidents that stands out in my mind involved my son, Alex, who was about three or four years old at the time.

I was stopping by my stepsister Julie's house just for a minute to pick something up. She lived in a log home up on a mountainside, and there was a very long driveway that led directly up to the side of her deck. At the bottom of the driveway was the road, and across the road, there was a drop off into a field.

Alex was in the back seat of the car in his car seat when I pulled up to the edge of the deck. I put the car in park and stepped directly onto the deck to get the item from Julie. All of a sudden, the car started rolling backwards down the driveway.

I ran as fast as I could and was almost at the door when I tripped and fell. Every imaginable thought ran through my mind in just a few seconds when I realized that at that point, I would not be able to catch the vehicle. I was watching my son going backwards down the driveway… and there wasn't anything that I could do about it. Time seemed to stand still.

Julie was also running towards the car. Within just a few moments, it was nearing the bottom of the driveway… when all of a sudden, the wheel turned abruptly; and the car started going backwards back up the hill onto the lawn. Julie jumped into the car and went to put it in park, but when she did, she found that it already was in park!

I was beyond relieved… there were just no words… I was just thanking God for sparing my son.

But it wasn't until later when Alex said the most astounding thing to me that I realized the extent of what had happened that day. He asked me, "Mom, did you see the angel that turned the wheel?" I was in shock! What little boy of that age would think to make something like that up? God had sent an angel to spare my son!

Over the years, I have thought of this now and then; and each time that I think of it, I am reminded of the love of my Father in Heaven for Alex and me, and for the plans He has for each of my children's lives. The Word of God says that angels are His messengers and that He dispatches them to watch over and protect us.

For He shall give His angels charge over you,
Psalm 91:11 (NKJV)

Please know that there is so much more going on around us in the spirit realm that we cannot see with the naked eye. There are angels, and there are demonic spirits as well. However, we know Who is directing the angels to watch over us; and when we dwell in the "secret place" of the Most High, we abide in the Shadow of the Almighty, and we can put our confidence in all of God's promises.

He who dwells in the secret place of the Most High shall abide under the shadow of the Almighty.
Psalm 91:1 (KJV)

Reverend Pamela Bolton, *Pastor, Author, and Revivalist*
Out of the Box Worship Center and First Baptist Church
Whitehall, New York

Day 11

From Intoxicated to Liberated!

***Stand fast therefore in the liberty by which Christ has made us free, and do not be entangled again with a yoke of bondage.* Galatians 5:1 (KJV)**

I can't count on my fingers and toes how many times I have heard the spiel about how Jesus saves. When I was 14 and my mom went to prison after several small-time incarceration sentences, I had decided the church had no place for me and Jesus didn't care if I was there or anywhere else for that matter. So let me make it clear: I did not believe in the wonder working power of Jesus Christ. Period!

My childhood was surely not the worst, but it was toxic; and drug and alcohol abuse were normalized. Despite my best efforts at chasing the American dream, I fell into the same familial bondage. Years of chronic physical and emotional pain left me empty inside, and I tried to chase away the emptiness with all the drugs and alcohol money could buy.

By age 27, I was managing my drug addiction but still feeling hollow and hopeless. I had become dependent on pornography, sexual encounters, my prescriptions, and cigarettes. I realized that I had become a totally functioning alcoholic. The functioning part honestly scared me the most....

While browsing the internet in a drunken stupor for another hookup, I came across a gentleman who wanted to talk to me about the church he served in. I was convinced it was an act and made it clear I didn't want commitment. I was stunned that he responded with the notion that he was looking for commitment. We stopped talking but followed one another on social media, and contrary to what had become my typical behavior, I felt something was wrong, so I checked on him. That action led me down an unexpected trajectory....

In the early months of our relationship, my boyfriend had told me about his Salvation. He told me of his personal struggles and how he served in ministry. I took much of it lightly, because he was right there with me in sin. Eventually, I followed him to church to claim my first victory in Christ, and while this victory is in no way to be taken lightly, I want to tell everyone I can that even *chemical dependency* is NO MATCH FOR MY GOD!

I learned from my then boyfriend of testimonies about people who had been healed instantly. It was just like in the Bible when the lame would walk and the blind would see, yet there I was drinking away every penny I had. I never went to bed at a normal hour. I was drinking on my way home from work and lying to my family; I realized I had to give it up. I had given up other stuff, and this needed to go too. That was three large bottles of wine, three 24 oz. beers, and five small liquor shooters per day…. The alcohol no longer mattered to me. As if it were that easy…! If there is one thing that has been determined about alcoholism, it's that you do NOT get to decide when it's over.

At first, I tried to drink a little less each day, but I always went into the next day's supply. Then I tried a day's supply at a time, but I always went to get more. Finally, I thought that just maybe if I bought booze that I didn't like... that didn't work either. I was hopeless. Every waking hour of every day, all I could think of was whether or not I had enough money for one of those high content beers... just one!

I convinced my boyfriend that I was successful and started sneaking a drink on my drive home from work. He thought my good mood was because of an affair, so I broke down and told him about how I had been drinking on my commute. He prayed with me, and the next day, I went without a drink! Finally!

That night I didn't sleep. The next day, I had chills and was shaking uncontrollably. I called into work sick. The next night, I didn't sleep again. The next day, I thought I felt better and was thrilled about day three and celebrated with a drink, "just one for my shift."

That weekend, the landlord came with an eviction notice. As soon as he left, I mustered up the money needed for a six-pack. There is always money for the devil! I started getting sloppy in my work, and people were noticing. My children had begun asking what was happening as life began to crumble around me... around us!

This time I slowly weaned myself off... it was either that or homelessness. I had lost my job but found another. I was not sleeping, and my relationships were suffering. I didn't want to be around my kids, and even church was a burden. I was back to feeling empty… even after tasting how good God was!

One day, while alone at my new job, I crossed the street for lunch. I left with a beer to fill that emptiness. I drank it on the clock, and the cycle began again.

I was a slave. I always wondered if the police knew. Would my boss show up? Will I be able to drive in this snowstorm? Can the clients smell it on my breath? None of my fears changed my decision to drink. I was even warned by my doctor that my meds mixed with alcohol was lethal; I was committing suicide daily. And I was okay with it, because I was powerless… fighting monsters that I could not see; but Jesus wanted to step in!

One Saturday, on my way to work, I quickly guzzled down a 24 oz. beer on a back road. I was abruptly struck with pain so unbearable that I could not drive. I was right at a police speed check and petrified, but the pain exceeded my fear by a longshot. I cried out, "JESUS, I AM SORRY. PLEASE HELP!"

Isn't that the way? When we are desperate, we really beg! I had begged for help before, and He showed up. Then, I was crying not for sobriety but for MERCY!

I felt urged to make myself vomit... strange... but when I did it, the pain ceased *immediately*. I spent my entire shift contemplating how I could face the pain of alcohol detox again, now that I had failed a third time. The fevers, chills, and digestive disfunction... I did not have it in me to do this, but that pain and immediate recovery were no joke. I needed to pay attention to what was happening.

When I got home from work, I went into the tiny, closet-sized bathroom in my apartment. One or all of my boys had missed the toilet, and the floor was a mess. It was on that very floor that I first placed my face to the floor and cried out, "Jesus, I have heard a million stories of how you brought people into recovery overnight. Kim Walker Smith was set free from meth; the founder and lead guitarist from Korn was delivered from hard drugs. Jesus, I need that. Please do this for me, too, Jesus. I'm sorry, Jesus. Please don't leave me like this. Please, Jesus. Please, Jesus. If these stories are real, please, Jesus. I have nothing to give you, but I know I need this. Please, Jesus. Please, Jesus. Please, Jesus. Please, Jesus." By the time I finished praying... pleading... sobbing, I was physically and emotionally exhausted. I smelled of urine and knew I wouldn't be able to sleep with no alcohol in my system. I got up off the floor, washed my face, whispered, "I love you, Jesus," and went into my bedroom.

I don't remember falling asleep. But I remember waking up and not thinking about beer. I remember going to church and not shaking. My belly didn't grumble, and I did not run off after service.

That day was April 14, 2018. On April 20, 2018, I got pulled over on my drive to work. I found out that I had no driver's license, and the inspection on the vehicle I had borrowed was expired. By the grace of the One and Only, Jesus Christ, I was NOT driving under the influence or with an open container.

It was by His stripes that I was healed when I least expected it. Though I may have let Him down *every single day*, He came for me. He comes for me every single time, no matter how short I fall of all expectation. You see the scripture is true; Romans 5:8 says, "But God demonstrates His own love toward us, in that while we were still sinners, Christ died for us (NKJV)." There is not a day that has passed that I did not cling to this love and pray that others would recognize it too.

I spent so much time envying those who had been healed. I deemed myself unworthy, but the fact is that Jesus Christ wants to leave the 99 to come find you. Jesus wants to see your radical healing, your victory. He wants to be your testimony *more* than you actually want the thing you have been desiring to be set free from! If you think you can't be set free from whatever has you bound, that's a lie from the enemy. John 8:36 says, "...if the Son makes you free, you shall be free indeed (NKJV)."

This freedom found in Jesus Christ brought me to life for the first time. I started with addiction on top of addiction, but today, I am married to the man who introduced me to Jesus, sober, and headed into eternity by the Grace of God. John 10:28 says, "I give unto them eternal life and they shall never perish, neither shall any man pluck them out of my hand (KJV)."

No matter where you have been, what you have done, or what you are addicted to, Jesus is waiting to hear you cry out. Open your heart to Him, and let no one and *nothing* tear you away from the abundant life that He wants you to live. I am still sober, and I could not say that if it weren't for the living God who saved my soul when He bore my sin and shame on the cross! Hallelujah! If He would help me when I cried out to Him, He will help you, too!

***Rae Lee Geertgens**, Jesus Enthusiast*
Southern Vermont

DAY 12

GOD OF THE IMPOSSIBLE!

***But He said, "The things which are impossible with men are possible with God."* Luke 18:27 (NKJV)**

I truly stand in awe of God and all He has done in my life and the lives of those I love! When people tell me that God doesn't speak to them, my response is, "God is speaking to you, but you just don't want to hear what He's saying!" Early in my walk, it took me a season to trust that what I was "hearing" was actually coming from God. And even now, I ask Him to confirm important words and promises that He speaks to me.

I am reminded of Gideon in the Book of Judges, who asked God on several occasions to perform special signs so that he would know that it was truly God speaking to him. Judges, Chapter 6, says:

So Gideon said to God, "If You will save Israel by my hand as You have said—look, I shall put a fleece of wool on the threshing floor; if there is dew on the fleece only, and it is dry on all the ground, then I shall know that You will save Israel by my hand, as You have said." And it was so. When he rose early the next morning and squeezed the fleece together, he wrung the dew out of the fleece, a bowlful of water. Then Gideon said to God, "Do not be angry with me, but let me speak just once more: Let me test, I pray, just once more with the fleece; let it now be dry only on the fleece, but on all the ground let there be dew." And God did so that night. It was dry

on the fleece only, but there was dew on all the ground.
Judges 6:36-40 (NKJV)

In May of 2019, the Lord spoke to me about going to India as an evangelist and missionary, but I wasn't sure that it was really God who was speaking to me. I asked Him to confirm to me that He was sending me to India, because I had received several invitations through social media to go on crusade there to speak to the people, encourage them in the Lord, and spread the Gospel. I took a step of faith and completed the necessary paperwork online for a visa to India on their government website. I completed the application on Saturday morning around 11 AM CST, USA, May 11, 2019, which was the Saturday before Mother's Day. Now, I realized that India was around twelve hours ahead of the time where I lived, which meant that it was Saturday evening in India. I completed the application honestly, and I was asked on the visa application if I was of the Christian faith, and of course I answered, "Yes"!

I really didn't expect that the visa would be accepted, especially since the Government of India is anti-Christian. I prayed and told the Lord that if He was calling me to India, then He would make sure that the visa was approved. I didn't go as far as Gideon did in asking for a sign, but I did ask God to confirm His word to me. So imagine my surprise when I was checking my e-mail Sunday morning, Mother's Day, May 12, 2019, around 8 AM CST, USA. I had received an e-mail from the Government of India stating that my visa application had been approved! What?! My mouth was just standing open, and I was in complete awe and wonder. God confirmed to me that He was sending me to India! My visa application was approved in less than 24 hours, on a weekend for both countries and a holiday weekend on top of that! What's impossible with man, is possible with God, indeed!

I believe that we have to activate our faith when God gives us a word or a promise. The Book of James says, "For as the body without the spirit is dead, so faith without works is dead also (James 2:26, KJV)."

What promise has God given you? Maybe you don't even believe it's God speaking to you. But, just as I did and just as Gideon did, if you are not sure it's God speaking to you, then ask Him to confirm it for you; and believe me, He will! But your part is to act in faith, trust Him, and believe Him at His word. Jesus said to the father of the son oppressed by a demon:

> ***"If you can believe, all things are possible to him who believes."***
>
> ***Immediately the father of the child cried out and said with tears, "Lord, I believe; help my unbelief!"***
> **Mark 9:23-24 (NKJV)**

Lord Jesus, as the man above prayed, I pray to You, Lord, help our unbelief, for surely all things are possible for us when we believe!

Sonia Lott, MD, *Minister, Intercessor, Healer/Physician, and Speaker Founder/Lead Minister of Face 2 Face Global Inc.*
Host of the radio show #TRUTH w/Dr. Sonia
Chicago, Illinois

Day 13

Divine Encounter

He that dwelleth in the secret place of the most High shall abide under the shadow of the Almighty.
Psalm 91:1 (KJV)

Experiencing the realm of the supernatural and divine angelic encounters can be life changing. God is supernatural, and every Christian should walk and embrace the supernatural aspect of His nature. Exactly a decade ago, I experienced one divine encounter that changed my life forever.

I grew up in a Christian home, and I remember having a desire to serve God; but somewhere along the way, my faith became more "religious," than about having a passionate relationship with Jesus. There were points in my life when my fervent love for God was real. He actually manifested His love towards me many times since I was a little girl.

How do I know that? When God was calling me, I asked Him, "LORD, if I ever loved you, please take me to that very place where I met you for the first time in my life." Amazing and loving as He is, in my mind, He brought me back to the little church where I used to go with my grandfather. The change started right there, when He took me back in time and showed me, like a picture, an image of me among the people in the church worshipping and praising Him. That moment was just the beginning of a true adventure with Him.

I had walked away from my Christian life for a while. I was confused about some things about God and the way many Christians lived their lives. I also questioned Him about things that had happened to me in the past. I never blamed God, but I didn't believe that "real" Christians even existed. I never doubted the existence of God, but I thought that He was high and unreachable. If the people who were always preaching and talking about Him couldn't keep perfection and holiness, then how could I even dream of walking anywhere close to Him?

In the midst of my struggles, one day I told God that I didn't know what to believe; but I did know that He was calling me. His voice started sounding stronger, and finally, I surrendered. I let go of my resistance and cried out to Father God to bring me back home. I visited Christian churches of different denominations. I attended the Catholic Church for close to a decade, while attending a non-denominational Christian church at the same time. I was trying to find my place but not taking it as seriously as I should have.

Easter Sunday of April 2011 was the day that I learned that my time of playing church had to stop. The non-denominational church had announced the prior week that their Easter service would start earlier, but since I missed that service, I didn't hear that it was starting early. I arrived late, just as the service was ending, and I will never forget the look on the face of the lady pastor… Wow!

When God is dealing with our character, it is better to be ready. Three days after this, things would never be the same for me and my family.

On Wednesday, April 27th, 2011, I woke up just like on any other day. (We had been living in Harvest, Alabama, for about five years at that time.) I got ready to go to work, and I took my kids to school. When I got to work, I met my first client in the parking lot; and she mentioned that she was from Arkansas. She told me to look up at the sky. As I lifted up my head to look, she proceeded to explain to me that the way the clouds were moving indicated that a tornado was forming. Less than a half hour later, the school called to inform me that I needed to pick up my children. I didn't even have time to finish my client's hair.

My children's schools were in three different locations. While driving to pick up my son, I saw what looked like a black curtain in front of me. The tornado had touched the ground. Immediately, I turned to my right side and drove away from it. The inevitable happened; the tornado reached me. I couldn't see the road, and as the debris, tree branches, and hail hit my car, fear took over. I knew that I was in serious danger.

> ***Train up a child in the way he should go, and when he is old he will not depart from it.*** **Proverbs 22:6 (KJV)**

I began to pray as my mother had taught me to and proclaim Psalm 23, which I had memorized as a child. How powerful the Word of God is! Prayer really opens Heaven. Finally, I was able to see my way out, and I picked up my kids, one at a time, from their respective schools.

When I got home, I prepared to possibly leave the house since there were more tornadoes coming in our direction. At that very moment, I received a message from my friend who warned me about another tornado that was on its way, stronger than the one that hit me on the road; and she told me that it would possibly hit our house.

I tried to find shelter for my kids and myself in the hallway. We sat there with pillows and blankets. I prayed with them and read Psalm 91; then I put my Bible on the dining room table and went back into the hallway.

Immediately, another tornado (rated EF5) touched the ground. I surrounded my children the best that I could with my arms. The tornado hit our house, and the loud noise was very frightening. My daughters started screaming in horror. It was real! *How is this possible?* I thought… *not again!* I cried out to

God once more, "LORD, please forgive me. I know that I have not been faithful to You as I should have been."

At the same time, my mind repeatedly was saying, *This is it! You will die today, and you will not go to a good place!* How painful that is… thinking that you may die and that your life is not straight with God.

I thought about my kids, and I asked God to protect them. I was so scared. I didn't want to die.

In the moment when my hope was failing, my son lifted up his head and said, "We're not going to die. We have a mission to fulfill." It was like he could hear what I was thinking.

At that very moment, I also lifted up my head, and as I looked up, I saw the attic door fly away. Then I turned my head to the right, and as I did, I heard a soft voice like a whisper say, "This doesn't last long." At the same time that I looked to the side, I saw what I would describe as an angel, with a bright white glowing tunic, that reached from the floor and passed up through the ceiling. It was like our house had no roof. That's the only way I can describe what I saw. The angel was so tall that I couldn't see his face, but I knew he was there, right beside me!

Then peace invaded my heart and mind, peace that is indescribable. I felt that peace that surpasses all understanding. All fear and thoughts that I would die suddenly dissipated. When I tried to look up with my eyes to see the angel, in less than seconds, he was gone.

After such an amazing encounter, I really understood that my God and Father truly covered me under His wings like He promised in Psalm 91. My mind changed from being afraid to singing a song. The lyrics go like this: "You are my Strong Tower, Shelter over me, beautiful and mighty Everlasting

King…." (Kutless). At that moment, I knew that God was there the whole time. The tornado only lasted less than a minute, although it felt like an eternity.

I later learned that 253 Alabamians lost their lives in the tornadoes that touched down that day, including the father of one of my daughter's best friends. We knew the family very well, and he was the person who normally drove her to school each day.

God has promised us that He will turn our mourning into dancing, and He will gird us with gladness (Psalm 30:10). We may weep and lament and grieve, but God will turn our sorrow into joy.

> ***Most assuredly, I say to you that you will weep and lament, but the world will rejoice; and you will be sorrowful, but your sorrow will be turned into joy.***
> **John 16:20 (NKJV)**

God manifested His presence and glory to me that day, and He changed the way I saw Him. I felt loved, and I learned that when His children cry out to Him, He runs to save them. Prior to this experience, I think I had never recognized just how big His love is.

Angels of God are messengers, and God sends them to Earth to deliver messages from Heaven. When we pray, God in Heaven hears our requests. From the very moment we place our petition for something that is in accordance with the will of the Father, the command goes out from the throne of our God. In that very moment, God dispatches His angels to work on behalf of our plea.

> ***Yes, while I was speaking in prayer, the man Gabriel, whom I had seen in the vision at the beginning, being caused to fly swiftly, reached me about the time of the***

evening offering. And he informed me, and talked with me, and said, "O Daniel, I have now come forth to give you skill to understand. At the beginning of your supplications the command went out, and I have come to tell you, for you are greatly beloved; therefore consider the matter, and understand the vision:
Daniel 9:21-23 (NKJV)

Every single sincere prayer is important to God, and every single one of them reaches Heaven. Revelation 5:8 says, "Now when He had taken the scroll, the four living creatures and the twenty-four elders fell down before the Lamb, each having a harp, and golden bowls full of incense, which are the prayers of the saints (NKJV)."

Be encouraged… God knows all; He sees all; He hears your prayers, and He is always with you wherever you go!

Alma Patricia Medina*, Women's Ministry Director and Praise Dancer*
Ticonderoga Assembly of God and Out of the Box Worship Center
Ticonderoga and Whitehall, New York

Day 14

Encounter with the Healer

***What is man that You are mindful of him, And the son of man that You visit him? For You have made him a little lower than the angels, And You have crowned him with glory and honor.* Psalm 8:4-5 (NKJV)**

The doctor looked at me and said, “Your test came back positive for signs of cancer.” I had been through several tests over a period of time, and after the final one, I was presented with this diagnosis. I left the office, not really knowing how to feel. I was a naive young lady. To be honest, I don’t think it really phased me much nor did I understand the potential of this being something that could take my life.

A few weeks had passed, and our church was holding revival services. I almost didn’t go, but my husband and I felt a tug that maybe we should attend. Am I ever glad that we went, because the event that happened that evening changed my life forever.

After the time of worship, the evangelist went up and spoke for a few minutes. He hadn’t really begun his message yet, when he said that while he was in prayer for that night’s service, the Lord showed him a young lady who was just diagnosed with cancer. He went on to say, “You’re a shy person. Come up. The Lord wants to heal you.”

I looked around the room watching for some other person to get up, but nobody did. After all, I was feeling like, *Who am I that the Lord would personally seek me out?* As I sat there, a feeling like a rushing wave touched me, and it was as if someone took me by the belt loop and lifted me up out of my seat. I stood up and walked down the aisle.

I heard a few people in the congregation gasp in surprise. I had not told anyone what the doctor had said, not even my mother or my husband at this point. The Lord certainly did reveal it that evening!

As I began walking down the aisle, the evangelist said, "Ah, yes, it's you," as if confirming what the Lord had shown him earlier in his time of prayer. As I stood in front of him, I felt an electric feeling through my body. He just barely laid his hand over me to pray, and I was down on the floor; and I remained there for several minutes.

A few more weeks had gone by when I decided to go see my grandmother for the night. She lived about an hour and a half away.

At about 9:30 PM, I began having horrible cramps. They would come and go as the night went on, and like contractions, they could be timed. It was 4:00 AM when I felt like I had to push as if I was in labor, but knew I wasn't pregnant. As I pushed, my body expelled a mass of tissue. I then woke up my grandmother, and she suggested I save it and take it to a doctor for testing. My husband and mother were called in the morning to drive me home.

The following business day, the doctor's office told me where to bring the specimen and made a follow-up appointment for me.

They tested the specimen, and during the appointment, the doctor gave me the lab results. There was no longer any evidence of cancer. This was the moment when I had to tell him my story about what took place at the revival service and how this came to be. I told him that Jesus had healed me. As he was turning to grab my paperwork off the table, I saw him crinkle his face and roll his eyes a little. I said, "I know this sounds strange. You said I have cancer, and now, you're saying I don't. I'm telling you that I know what happened. I cannot deny it, no matter how crazy it sounds."

I left the doctor's office astonished at what the Lord had done for me. He truly cared enough to heal me. He provided what I needed.

I wondered about the doctor and still do. I know he is still seeing patients. What seeds were planted that day? I know the Lord wastes nothing. With what happened, I believe that God was trying to reach out to that doctor, too.

I have learned that the Lord is very watchful, caring, and loving with His children. He doesn't miss anything in our lives, and He loves you as much as He loves me. Do you believe this? If God could do it for me, He can do it for you too!

> ***What is man that You are mindful of him, And the son of man that You visit him? For You have made him a little lower than the angels, And You have crowned him with glory and honor.*** **Psalm 8:4-5 (NKJV)**

***Evie Dean**, Pastor's Wife and Missionary to Kenya*
Mount Zion Church
Gansevoort, New York

Day 15

God's Faithful Deliverance in The Midst of Evil

"He will call upon Me, and I will answer him; I will be with him in trouble, I will rescue him and honor him."
Psalm 91:15 (AMP)

It was Friday, my youngest daughter and I arrived at Liberty University to move her into her dorm room. We made the drive from Upstate NY in her car. I'd help her move in, decorate her room with her, and fly back to Albany Sunday night. She was recovering from a long summer of Mononucleosis, and I was hoping she would take it easy and not overdo it at the beginning of the semester.

As for me, I had been feeling awful. My throat had been sore on and off for a few weeks. I was utterly exhausted and felt like I couldn't drink enough coffee during the day. I guess it was the busyness of the last few weeks. I made a mental note to see the doctor first thing Monday morning.

"You have Mononucleosis," the doctor said. What? I just had Mono at 47, a few years ago, after the same daughter had gotten it that summer, too. Now again, at 50 years old, here I was…, "You need to rest, cancel your schedule, drink lots of fluids, and have no physical activity." I was a regular jogger, but the doctor said, "Do nothing that causes any physical impact."

What a bummer, so I went home to rest for the week.

My nail technician texted me Wednesday evening and asked me if I could switch my Thursday appointment to an hour earlier and arrive at 3:30 PM. One of the elderly clients needed my time slot, which was a later appointment.

"No problem, my schedule is clear anyway. See you tomorrow at 3:30 PM," I sent back. The doctor had said that I wasn't actively contagious, and based on my symptoms, I was probably already three weeks into the process. I just needed rest and fluids.

That humid August Thursday morning, I got up and headed into my prayer time, like I always do. But that day, I was heavily impressed to pray longer in the Spirit. I had a burden on my heart that I couldn't shake. Something wasn't right. Something was very, very wrong.

Was it one of my children? Was it my husband? Extended family?

I knew I was interceding for something or someone; I was covering something in prayer. After an hour, I decided to get a booklet off the shelf in my bedroom, 94 Life and Strength Scriptures. The little booklet was easily ten years old. But I was drawn to it and went outside and began to walk around declaring the scriptures out loud, intermittently praying in tongues. I turned and looked at the sky; dark storm clouds were gathering. The air was heavy and humid, but the clouds looked very ominous.

Lord, what are you trying to say to me? What is it?

"I will not fear what befalls others!" I said loudly into the atmosphere, not knowing why I said that.

A short time later, I felt a peaceful release. I headed into the house, ate lunch, and got ready to go to the salon. My playlist was on repeat, and Hillsong Worship's "So Will I (100 Billion X)" echoed throughout my car. "If the stars are made to worship, so will I... If creation sings your praises, so will I...."

Denise was unusually quiet. We weren't good friends at the time. Our conversations were lighthearted and revolved around our kids, fun local restaurants, and lately, we had often talked about Fleetwood Mac's tour. They were coming to the Upstate New York area. We had talked about how fun it would be to see them in person for our 50th birthdays. My birthday was earlier in the summer, and hers was the next day! But the concert tour would feature great songs we both remembered fondly from our high school days.

Today though, there was none of that. She was quiet, somewhat distant, and preoccupied. I had no idea she was under tremendous emotional stress. I didn't know she had separated from her husband and that she was fearing for her life and afraid for her children. I didn't know there was a standing "Order of Protection and Stay Away" in place.

I watched a man in a baseball cap walk by the all-glass front windows to the front door. The salon had two main rooms in the front of the building—the hair salon side and the manicure/pedicure room. The hair salon was packed that day, and there were a lot of customers, but our room was quiet. Only Denise and I were in there.

Suddenly, the man I had just seen walk by, walked into the room and began to yell obscenities at Denise. I saw brass knuckles fitted on one hand and a knife in the other. In an instant, he violently yanked her small framed body out of the chair and plunged the knife into her.

I jumped out of my chair and yelled to call 911. I immediately scanned the room for something to fight him off with, and Denise's screams were piercing. I grabbed a rod iron dress form mannequin and sprinted back into the manicure room. I hit the attacker hard on his back!

"In the name of Jesus! In the name of Jesus, you stop it right now." BAM! I hit him again.

He looked stunned and froze for a split second. I could see Denise was not moving. Blood was pooling around her. He lunged at me with the knife. I kept the mannequin between us and hit him again, as hard as I could.

"In Jesus' name, I bind you Satan. You stop right now." BAM! I hit him again. I hit him every time he tried to look Denise's way. I wouldn't let him touch her. He lunged at me; I hit him. We repeated this over and over, as I shouted the name of Jesus.

But, after repeated blows, the mannequin broke in half. The bottom dropped off, and I was only left with the top and its pointed end that was supposed to fit into the base.

A point! I thought… *Jab it into his right temple. Aim for his temple!*

I aimed for the temple and missed. I hit him in the neck. He swung at me again. I tried one more time and yelled, "In Jesus' name, I bind you. Get out of here, Satan!"

The attacker looked confused and shoved me back hard. I hit the wall. I felt the blow to my back, and I dropped the top of the mannequin.

Get up, Liz. Hurry. Don't let him get you with the knife. Fight. Don't let him get Denise.

My shoes were sliding as I was trying to scramble to my feet. I was wearing flat dress shoes with a summer denim shirt dress. I couldn't get a good grip on my feet. The barbicide jar with all the manicure utensils had crashed to the floor. Nail polish bottles and nail polish remover were littered all over, and pieces of glass were everywhere. There was also a lot of blood.

Is she alive? My God... she's not moving. Jesus. Jesus. Jesus!

Someone's arms helped me up from behind. A woman's voice yelled from behind me. I grabbed hold of the manicure table and rammed it as hard as I could into the attacker's legs. He pushed it back into mine. We shoved the heavy table into each other's legs and went back and forth. I could feel the impact into my kneecaps with each blow. I could feel myself getting tired. I was putting all of my strength into each strike, and I felt myself weakening. I winced.

My God, where are the police? Please Jesus. God, help!

I knew the police were on their way. I knew multiple people in the salon were calling 911. I could see all the women in the parking lot in front of the building. They were frantic. Shocked. Terrified. *Fight, Liz. Fight.*

The voice from behind me was one of the owners of the salon. She yelled to the attacker. "Think of your kids! What are you doing?"

In that split second, he engaged with the owner. He yelled back to her.

Run, Liz. Run. Get more help. Run!

"I'm getting more help," I yelled. "We need help!" I ran outside into the parking lot and jumped up and down on the side of the road, waving my arms. A man in a pickup truck sitting at the red light, immediately turned into the lot and jumped out of his car. “He’s trying to kill her,” I screamed! “Help! He’s trying to kill her!”

The large, very muscular man, well over 6’ tall, ran in the front door. I ran right behind him. By the time I ran around the corner into the manicure room, this man had the attacker in a massive choke hold, and the attacker dropped the knife and brass knuckles.

I ran to Denise, dropped to the floor and picked up her head and cradled her in my arms. There was no sign of life. She was completely ashen grey. Her eyes were opened and off to the side, fixed. There was no blinking. No movement. She seemed gone. She was limp, appeared lifeless and in a pool of blood. *Jesus! Jesus! Jesus!* My hands cupped her cheeks, and I put my mouth to her ear.

“Denise. Denise, I know you can hear me. In the name of Jesus, right now I take authority over every wound, every injury, and I command all bleeding to cease and desist right now in the name of Jesus. I decree and declare you shall live and not die. You shall live and not die in the name of Jesus. I take authority over every wound and all trauma, and I command healing right now. Every wound be bound and healed. All trauma, GO, in Jesus’ name. You will live. You will be okay. Do you understand, Denise? You will be okay. In Jesus’ name.”

Just then, another man appeared at my side in the room. He had a walkie talkie clipped to his shoulder. “Expedite the ambulance. Expedite the ambulance.” He looked at me and calmly said. “I need you to help me. Can you do that? I need you to get me wet towels.”

I jumped up, threw the pedicure towels into the foot tub, rung them out quickly, and gave them to him. He was feeling for a pulse, and he placed the towels on her shoulder, which was very badly torn; ligaments and muscle were easily visible.

There was no skin. Then he carefully placed additional towels on her abdomen.

At that moment it seemed as if all the police cars arrived at once, along with the ambulances. I don't recall how many there were, but there were a lot. An officer gently lifted me from under my arm.

"Ma'am? Ma'am, are you okay? Do you need medical help?" I couldn't understand why the EMT's were waiting outside the big glass window. *Why aren't they rushing in here?* I would later learn that the officers had to secure the building first. They had no idea what they were walking into or if there was more than one attacker.

The building was swarming with officers. The sirens seemed to never stop. There was a forensic truck and ambulances waiting on the scene. The police officer very gently let me know I couldn't talk to anyone. He said I needed to sit in the police car. Before he escorted me to the police cruiser, he helped me call my husband and asked him to meet us at the station. As I walked with the officer to the police car, I asked one of the owners who was standing in the parking lot, "Who was that guy?" I learned it was Denise's estranged husband.

God, she has to live. She must live. Jesus, Jesus, Jesus.

Hours later, we returned home. We called our pastors, and they prayed over me, as well as Denise. I learned over the next 24 hours, that Denise endured two major life saving trauma surgeries, and she had lost over two liters of blood during the attack. I also learned that her estranged husband sliced a 13" knife wound across her abdomen, exposing her intestines. But she was alive.

On Saturday, I went to the hospital and was able to see her. She was miraculously alive and slowly eating ice chips. We had an emotional visit. She was in and out of a sedated sleep. But, by Monday, she was walking around the nurses' island! By Thursday, she was home with her children. Six weeks later, Denise was back at work in the salon.

To this day, she doesn't remember the details of the traumatic and violent salon attack in August of 2018. As a matter of fact, she sits in the same place, same chair and uses the same desk. She doesn't recall what happened. Just as I prayed, the Lord answered. She has made a full physical recovery. I also had the honor of leading her daughter to the Lord, and she received Jesus Christ as Savior.

Following the attack, I received a phone call from my doctor's office. "The Mononucleosis blood work shows no Mono present or past," the nurse said.

"What do you mean no past? I had it at 47, three years ago."

"Yes, I see that. It's in the medical records here. But your blood work shows otherwise. There is no past Mono and no present Mono in any of your blood work," she said.

"So, you're saying I don't have Mono now? And, I never had Mono? Is that right?"

"That's what the blood work says," she said.

"I'll take that report," I said. "That's great news."

I hung up the phone. My wrists, knees, and back were bruised and sore from the attack. *Lord, you healed me, didn't you?*

Just then, I heard Leviticus 17:11 in my spirit: *The life is in the Blood. Because you saved the life blood of another, I have redeemed yours. The blood speaks. The blood cries out.*

The Lord redeemed my past blood work. He healed me in the present of Mononucleosis, and He also went back and redeemed the blood from a past diagnosis. My blood work now shows no past Mono, ever!

At the one-year anniversary of the salon attack, Denise and I purposely scheduled our appointment for the exact time and date. We have taken back what the enemy tried to steal, kill, and destroy that day. In the midst of that evil attack, the name of Jesus was being shouted and called upon. He was faithful to deliver.

As Christians, we are going to find ourselves increasingly in the midst of darkness, especially in the time we are living in. We must stay attached to the Lord… listening and discerning. God orders our steps. He may purposely position you in the midst of evil, but He will also equip you so you are enabled to do what He needs you to do. A beautiful woman is alive and well, with her children, because of the power of prayer the morning of the attack. I could have ignored the Spirit's leading that morning, but I didn't. I want to always be sensitive to listen. I pray that I am.

I'm doing well. Denise is doing well. Her children are doing well. Her estranged husband is serving 25 years in Great Meadow Correctional Facility, maximum security prison, in Comstock, NY. I have forgiven him, and I pray that he will be saved and come to a relationship with Jesus Christ.

God is faithful! Had the elderly woman been in that chair, instead of me, I don't think Denise would be here today. God knew, and He equipped. He will never leave us without the power of the Holy Spirit.

Liz Joy*, Candidate for Congress*
Schenectady, New York

Day 16

Secrets from the "Secret Place"

***The secret of the Lord is with those who fear Him, and He will show them His covenant.* Psalm 25:14 (NKJV)**

I like the way this verse is written in the Amplified Bible, Classic Edition. It goes like this:

The secret (of the sweet, satisfying companionship) of the Lord have they who fear (revere and worship) Him, and He will show them His covenant and reveal to them its (deep, inner) meaning.

According to *Strong's Concordance*, the word "SECRET" in Hebrew is "Cowd" (pronounced sōde). It means intimacy, intense counsel, to sit together, and/or to lay a foundation.

The Lord Most High, the King of Kings who shed His blood for us, desires to have an intimate relationship with each one of us who revere and worship Him. He wants to sit together with us and lay His foundation in each of our lives. He wants to share things with us… His secrets, His counsel, and His wisdom.

Jesus promised in John 14:15-16, "If you (really) love Me, you will keep (obey) My commands. And I will ask the Father, and He will give you another Comforter (Counselor, Helper, Intercessor, Advocate, Strengthener, and Standby) that He may remain with you forever—" (AMPC)

In Daniel 2:28, Daniel said, "But there is a God in Heaven who reveals secrets." In this Book, we are told that Daniel, along with many other young people were taken from their homeland of Judah, into Babylonian captivity. The lives of Daniel and his friends exemplified the utmost in faith, trust, and consecration to God. They were men of prayer and fasting, and God honored their faith by revealing His secrets to Daniel; miraculously protecting their lives; and performing miracles, signs, and wonders.

We are never wasting time when we spend time in the SECRET PLACE with the Lord and in His Word. It is when we do this, that His Spirit begins to change our hearts, mold us into His image, and birth in us the wisdom that we need, along with the very special gifts that He desires to impart and release within each one of us, which will bring glory to His name.

Many years ago, when I first began to understand that the Lord desired to have an intimate relationship with me, not just everyone else, I was excited.

Because I loved to worship the Lord in song, study His Word, pray, and just sit in His presence, I would do this for several hours at a time. Yes, sometimes the heavens felt like brass, and the enemy would try to tell me that I was wasting precious time. However, a season began where I would open the Word, and the Lord would birth a new song directly from the scriptures. He would often tell me what to read, and then He would inspire another song. He still does this as I commit myself to spending time with Him.

He has done this over and over again throughout the years. I get as excited today, as I did the first time that this happened. It is out of the SECRET PLACE, sitting in His presence and under His counsel, that He gives us His plans, His messages, and His ideas.

A number of years ago, we were in the process of building a church and had just broken ground. I became extremely anxious over the cost and responsibility. In fact, I became so anxious that I lost His peace. I prayed all night until early morning, when I finally fell asleep and had a dream. I dreamt that I was in the new building. Inside the front of the church, to the right, was a well of water. Standing beside it was a man in white (an angel) with a basket of bread, and he was feeding the fish.

After watching him do this all day, I said to him, "Excuse me, sir. Haven't they had enough? After all, there are only a few fish in there."

He looked at me with eyes that to this day, I cannot forget. He did not criticize my lack of faith. Instead, he said, "Let me show you something." Out of the floor, came a wall of water that went to the ceiling. In it were so many fat, healthy, and different colored fish, that I was not able to count them.

Immediately, I awoke and heard the Lord say, "Ezekiel 47:9." I grabbed the Bible and read, "And wherever the double river shall go, every living creature which swarms shall live. And there shall be a very great number of fish, because these waters go there that (the waters of the sea) may be healed and made fresh; and everything shall live wherever the river goes." (AMPC)

It became very obvious to me that the Lord knew what He was doing. It is often in remembering what He has revealed in secret that helps us to press on during seasons of difficulty.

When we were building, I had thought there was only going to be a few people who would attend the church. The dream revealed to me that God had a bigger plan than what I had imagined, and within a year of when the church was built, the congregation had doubled in size; and God was doing amazing things. When I read the scripture that the Lord gave to me, I knew that in time, we would begin to see an even greater dimension of God's healing take place in the lives of His people.

> ***"And it shall come to pass in the last days," says God, "that I will pour out my spirit on all flesh;"***
> **Acts 2:17 (NKJV)**

Donna LaPierre, *Licensed Minister, Musician, and Songwriter*
Kingsway Worship Center and Out of the Box Worship Center
Hudson Falls and Whitehall, New York

DAY 17

NEW WORDS IN AN OLD HOUSE

...for to one is given the word of wisdom through the Spirit, to another the word of knowledge through the same Spirit, to another faith by the same Spirit, to another gifts of healings by the same Spirit,
1 Corinthians 12:8-9 (NKJV)

I sure got my money's worth out of that old house on the hill. I moved in after I had been born again for about five years. The sprawling great room actually housed two different church Bible studies. When it was not convenient to use the church locations, they would move their pot luck suppers to my home, and the fellowship would go later into the evenings. I was blessed!

The landlord mowed the lawn, and that was about it. He was a missionary and spent much of his time traveling. I took care of everything else. After all, the rent was pretty easy to come up with, and it was easy to scrape and paint little sections of the exterior to keep the house looking fresh. I was never embarrassed.

I used the old, tired house to embrace my art students. I taught private lessons at the time, and my students had plenty of space to spread out with their canvases. The beehive continued for a few years like that until the Lord had a new level for me to advance to. I just could not see it at the time.

The doors of that dwelling opened up for new relationships in the body of Christ. One friendship that had developed over the years was with a lady named Linda. She had been a believer for much longer than yours truly. I respected her opinion. She had been through a lot, and this particular year was not any different.

PRAYER SESSION ONE

She made an appointment with me one day to come and discuss something very important. I had no clue what it was about, but I was honored that she would choose me to talk with about such an urgent subject. I opened the door and saw the trouble on her face. I knew that the discussion was going to be heavy.

Linda explained that a family member was missing in upstate New York. People had searched for this person but to no avail. We went into prayer right away, and the Lord showed me what had happened. The man had committed suicide by jumping off a bridge. I described the scene, and she confirmed the type of bridge and the country setting, as I told her what I was seeing supernaturally. I was just as shocked as she was!

I had been getting better and better at operating in my spiritual gift of the word of knowledge. The Lord had been training me for this gift while I was being saturated in prayer, almost every day in that old house. The word of knowledge came in bits and pieces, as I helped friends in prayer times at church, but there was never anything this heavy before. I wasn't sure if I liked the gift. Seeing these things in this depth wasn't what I signed up for, or so I thought.

PRAYER SESSION TWO

Linda called a few days later and wanted to come back. I dreaded it, and I did not want to take this on again. I knew, however, if I was the one who had had success with someone previously, I would logically go back for more help! I understood all of that. Even though it was a way to serve the Lord, it did not make me feel any better.

This time, her voice had more desperation in it! She relayed that they could not find the body. It was then I thought I was off the hook! I was in error over the whole thing and this would end session two!

Then the Lord showed me pictures again. The body was in a bend of the river near a place where there were old junk cars. At times when the river was high, some of the rusted, old junkers were covered with water. (Later, it was at this bend that his body was found, lodged in something and had remained fixed among the debris.) After that information, Linda did not stay long for chit chat, but hurried on her way.

As she went out the door, I saw another vision, this time with a warning. I told her that she'd better get into his house and look for a notebook type journal. In the journal, she would find all of the deceased man's notes and documentations of him being abused by relatives from an early age. If this leaked out into the wrong hands, it could be scandalous to her family. God was wanting to protect innocent family members from humiliation. Linda had no prior knowledge of the notebook or the contents, and she kept quiet to me about any rumored abuse from the past.

PRAYER SESSION THREE

More than a few days had past, and I was remembering supernatural details less and less. I went about my business with church activities and attempted gardening in the backyard. It needed a massive cleanup. Among the thorns and poison ivy, two giant rose bushes bloomed faithfully every year. They were so big and buggy! It took special clothing to approach their branches, to cut the dead heads off, and to energize those amazing bushes. I knew I had to do it. My mother was a great teacher when it came to the procreation of flowers, fruits, and vegetables. That Wisconsin farm gal never forgot what Gramps had taught her, and she passed it all on to me.

The phone rang, and it was Linda again. My heart sank. This time there was light in her voice combined with relief. When we sipped tea that afternoon, she encouraged me greatly. She and another family member had found the journal! The information in it was just too dark to share with anyone. We prayed with thanksgiving for what the Lord revealed to help with this investigation. I was relieved! It was over.

Linda and I remained friends for years after that but lost touch eventually, due to different courses of ministry that came our way. God gave me a traveling ministry, and she had a new family to care for. We would always love each other and spoke fondly to each other whenever our paths crossed.

I went forward with this word of knowledge gift, and it enhances my ministry today. The experience with Linda was the heaviest of all. I suppose it was so hard because the gifting was in its infancy at the time, and it was such a burden of information, but God knew I would be obedient.

Jesus reveals many things to me now. Most are strongholds in people. He has taught me "grace of speech" to be able to speak healing and deliverance into troubled souls, where they can receive it. For this, I am grateful.

***Patti Dahl**, Licensed Evangelist, Elder for the State of CT (Gospel Ministerial Alliance), and National Singer Songwriter Naugatuck, Connecticut*

Day 18

Love Like This

"But I say to you, love your enemies, bless those who curse you, do good to those who hate you, and pray for those who spitefully use you and persecute you that you may be sons of your Father in heaven; for He makes His sun rise on the evil and on the good, and sends rain on the just and on the unjust. For if you love those who love you, what reward have you? Do not even the tax collectors do the same? And if you greet your brethren only, what do you do more than others? Do not even the tax collectors do so? Therefore you shall be perfect, just as your Father in heaven is perfect."
Matthew 5:44-48 (NKJV)

It was heading towards the fall of the year 1999, when my husband and I decided it was time I took on a full-time job again. Our youngest son, Thomas, was entering 1st grade; and it was time for me to go back to the business world, as an administrative assistant. I was looking forward to the work and the money.

The night before we made this decision, I had a spiritual dream that I did not realize correlated with that decision. In the dream, I entered a large, elegantly decorated business office and found myself watching a young man, dressed in a suit, going through his workday. When I saw him, I thought, *He looks like my Thomas.* I was aware of his thoughts throughout the dream, which were centered on a relationship (with his girlfriend) that had just fallen apart. He had been harsh with her, which was the cause of the breakup. He was devastated about it and felt hopeless of ever having another chance with her, but even more so when, in his weakness, he had been enticed and gave way to an affair with another man. His thoughts were about how he was going to end the affair, but he felt intimidated by the man, and it seemed impossible to end it. In his desperation, he decided to end his life. I was beside him throughout the entire time, following his thoughts, but he was not aware of me at all. In time, the scene changed, and we were not in the office; we were inside his car. He was speeding down a road, purposely careening off the side, headlong, into a crash. The car turned end-over-end, and at the last moment, I heard him cry out for Jesus!

Immediately, the scene changed again. I was still with him, unnoticed. He was waking up on the bed in his childhood bedroom. His mom was calling him, “John, wake up, Honey, it's time to get up....” He was shocked... dumbfounded... looking around.

He responded to her, “Mom...?” but not loud enough for her to hear him. He was looking around his room amazed, feeling as though he was just given a second chance at life, beginning again from his days of innocence. He then noticed a stack of books on the windowsill at the head of his bed. He took hold of a children's Bible from the stack and turned to look at me, noticing me for the first time in the entire dream. He showed me his Bible and said, “I remember this; it's my Bible!” I had the sense that it had been important to him when he was young, and then I woke up.

To be honest, I never gave the dream another thought. In fact, it didn't come back to my mind at all for several days. I had not even seen any connection to it when, just moments after our discussion about me returning to the business world, our neighbor came by, and I shared the news with her about starting back to full-time work. She immediately said that her office was hiring a receptionist and offered to submit my resume to her office manager. And I still didn't see a connection when, within about a week, I started my new position at a posh insurance company! It all happened so fast!

I started on a Monday morning and was asked to join in on the office team meeting to meet all the players. I stood at the end of the table as each person, dressed in fine business suits, took their turn introducing themselves to me. Then it came around to a certain young man who introduced himself to me as John. I immediately thought, *He looks like my Thomas*, and it was at that moment, something clicked in my mind; and I suddenly saw everything just as it was in my dream. I realized the office, the décor, the man himself – all of it was just as it was in my dream... all of it!!! Except, I was not hearing his thoughts now, but I remembered them from the dream.

I returned to my receptionist desk and began to pray. I knew immediately I needed to pray that the Lord would open the door for me to become John's assistant. I knew now, without a doubt, that I was hired on by this company as an assignment for my real job, as a minister of the Kingdom of God.

I was at my receptionist position maybe a week or two at the most, when my office manager came to see me. She was apologetic when she explained that John's administrative assistant had been on maternity leave and decided not to return to the position. Our supervisor decided he wanted her to put me in that position temporarily. The job actually required special training, but they would not be able to provide that for me before I started, due to the immediate need. They asked if I would be willing to be thrown into the spot knowing nothing and learn as I go. Without hesitation, I said that I would be glad to help out! What they thought was a terrible thing to ask of me was actually my answered prayer! Praise the Lord!

For the next few weeks, I fumbled through the workload, doing tasks that I had no training for. I soon discovered firsthand the harsh treatment John's ex-girlfriend had experienced. Every day was full of cruel abuse by this young man. The other admins on staff were fully aware of his harshness, but I found an empty office and would take quick breaks to slip away unnoticed and fall on my face. I cried out to the Lord to give me grace to walk in love and forgiveness so that I would be effective for the work of the Kingdom at hand. I had the victory every day, but at the height of the abuse, one of the other admins reported what was happening to the office manager, who was so angry that she called a special meeting with the supervisor and me. They threatened to fire John in response to his actions. In fact, he was already in jeopardy of losing his job for his hot temper previous to my starting the job; but love filled my heart, and instead, I pleaded his case with them. They agreed to spare him, but at my first report of any more such treatment, he would be let go.

After the meeting, the young lady who reported John to the office manager came to me and told me about how she was abused at her previous job. She hated them for what they had done to her, and she finally left that job. She warned me not to put up with John's treatment. Mind you, I never accepted John's words like a whipped pup; I always held him accountable for how he treated me, much like a mother will do with her son. I assured her that I would work with John, and it would turn out well. “WHY? Don't you hate him?” she exclaimed. “How can I hate him when what he needs is love?” I blurted out from the bottom of my heart. I had discovered the Love of Christ for him shed abroad in my heart! It was a great victory!

During those weeks and in the hidden times of prayer, the Holy Spirit showed me that there was a call on this young man's life regarding the nation of Israel. He showed me there was a political position John was to fulfill in these last days. *That young man must live to fulfill that calling.* If I allowed offense to fill my heart, I would not be effective in my intercession for his life and calling or in ministering the word of God to him. The message I had for him from God was developing during that time, and finally, the opportunity to give it to him came as God was preparing his heart to hear and to receive it.

It was a Friday at quitting time. I was headed out the door when John called after me and asked if I would be willing to stay and put together a report that he needed for an important meeting that he was having that evening. He was not trained on the system I worked with, and I was not trained for the numbers that would be needed. He knew I owed him nothing, and this was a great opportunity to tell him "no" and where to go! But I knew it was the Lord working out the next move. So, I said that, yes, I'd help him but only if he would sit right with me and we'd work on it together. What could he say? So, he agreed!

I had his full attention now without anyone else in the office to overhear our conversation, so I could speak of personal information. The computer required us to input numbers and then wait a few minutes each time while it worked through the computations and set up the report. The whole process would take about an hour. So, slowly, in those waiting times, I began to speak. It started with him asking me why I wasn't trained for the position and why they hired me for it. I was able to say that I wasn't hired for that position, but as a receptionist, and that I had prayed for the opportunity to work with him because of a dream I had about him before I had ever met him and before I ever came to work there. He was shocked and wanted to know more. I did not feel comfortable telling him the details of the dream, but instead, I spoke to him the message the Lord had told me to share about his "call" in life. I told him how the Lord purposely sent me to him and that even the time we were spending together working on the report at that moment was ordained by God. As we sat there and talked, John's stony heart melted. He told me about how he used to have a love for God as a young boy (I knew this, of course, from my dream). He also told me that he went to college to enter a career in politics, but later he became disheartened and left that profession. By the time we finished that evening, John's life had changed. His attitude had changed and his regard for me had changed, too, when he realized that I had endured his abuse and didn't give up in order to reach him. The love of God at work in me, for him, was a wrecking ball that broke apart his encrusted heart.

For several weeks following that appointment with the Kingdom, I was able to speak to John on a daily basis. Each morning, I gave him encouragement and scriptures that were to open his understanding of the call on his life and his salvation. And then, just as abruptly as the Lord thrust me into that position, He removed me from it to go on to other things, other ministry. I believe I was with that company for a total of eight months.

Love is essential in the work of the Lord. Our love is proof to all who are watching that we have been in the presence of the Lord and that we belong to Him. It's the proof that we are truly the sons and daughters of God. If I had given way to temptation to protect myself from that young man's hateful words and attitude, I would have returned my own hot temper in response to his. And when the time came for me to deliver the message of God to him, it would have been ineffective and lacking regard. It was the love and the proof of it that was the sign and wonder that confirmed the word that I brought him was indeed from God. It captured his heart and redirected his life from destruction. Without maturing in the love of God, there is just a sounding gong, without value or merit to the sign and wonder. I should again say that I was not a doormat to his treatment. I made clear to him that he was not to speak to me as he did. I was firm and spoke the truth in love. He often would call to berate me in front of his meetings, and I made sure to tell him, much as a mother would say to a child, "I will speak to you when you get back to the office, John!" But, I continued in patience and not holding the wrong against him. It took humility before God and crying out in prayer to not allow offense to have its hold on me.

Often, it's these difficult occasions that are the opportunity for advancement and reward in the Kingdom. Opposition is often the impetus to maturity in our relationship with the Holy Spirit as we walk closely, following His every lead, remembering that the ones we would quickly disregard due to our flesh, He regards with such love and compassion beyond what we could ever understand. He longs to reach the unlovable; the ones we would rather have nothing to do with and we'd rather keep away from us, just as the other admin wanted to help me do. She meant well, and was still so hurt and scarred from her experience that she feared for me. But she didn't understand that I was learning to die to self, that Christ would live in me. I could not have done it in my flesh; it had to be done by His Spirit. Today, there is no scar, no hate... only a wonderful testimony of His great love and a brother in the Lord who was turned away from destruction.

S. L. Rogers*, Author of How to Pray and Receive from God*
and How to Hear the Voice of God
Shushan, New York

Day 19

Lovesick for You

***O God of my life, I'm lovesick for you in this weary wilderness.* Psalm 63:1 (TPT)**

One day while I was spending time with the Lord, He said to me, "Yong, I want you to open your Bible to John 3:16."

I said, "Lord, I know John 3:16."

He was silent. Then, He said again, "Yong, turn to John 3:16."

I said, "Lord, I know John 3:16. I don't have to open the Bible. I can just quote it to you."

He was silent. The third time, He said, "Yong, turn to John 3:16." I opened my Bible and read John 3:16 to Him.

***For God so loved the world, that he gave his only begotten Son, that whosoever believeth in him should not perish, but have everlasting life.* John 3:16 (KJV)**

Then He spoke and said, "Yong, I love you so much that I gave My one and only Son for you. Now, do you love me enough to give up your life for me?"

I didn't know what to say. I was undone. I sat there weeping and wanting to say "yes" immediately, but I thought, *What if I can't keep my promise to Him?* So, I sat there and wept and wept. I don't know for how long, but finally, I said, "Lord, I don't know what it all entails, but I say, 'Yes'." Then I asked Him, "Would you please help me to keep my promise to you?"

I grew up in South Korea, and I had never been to church or even heard the Gospel. I don't remember ever hearing John 3:16. No one ever told me about Jesus. When I was going through a very difficult time in my marriage, I didn't know where or who to turn to. I was very depressed, wanting to end my life. A friend came and talked to me about Jesus. Then, she took me to her friend's house. She read something out of a brown book (now I know it was a Bible). Then she told me, "pray." I had never heard about the salvation prayer. I didn't know how to pray, but I looked up to heaven and said something. Tears began to stream down my face. God understood my prayer. I gave my life to the Lord in February 1983; I knew I was changed!

I went to church every time the door opened. I wanted to learn all that I could about the Lord. I had to know this God whom I never knew or heard about before. So, I began to pursue Him. I fasted, prayed, studied the Word, and worshiped for hours every day, crying out for more of Him. I was like a hungry beggar in the streets.

One time, I fasted and prayed for 21 days, crying out to God just to know Him more. When I read books or listened to testimonies of people's encounters, I would cry out to Him for more. I couldn't even sleep. Sometimes I just waited for Him to come.

One morning as I was getting out of bed, the CD player began to play my favorite song, without me pushing the play button. I thought it was strange, but I sat down and got lost in worshipping Jesus. When the song was over, I got up to leave. The song played again. I sat down and worshiped the Lord. When the song ended, it began to play over again. I sat down and worshiped again. Then, I decided to check my CD player to see if it was stuck; it wasn't. Someone had to turn to track 6 and push the play button. Track 6 was my favorite song, "Even

So." The Lord was drawing and wooing me to be with Him by playing my favorite song.

> ***"Draw me into your heart. We will run away together into the king's cloud-filled chamber."***
> **Song of Songs 1:4 (TPT)**

John Fletcher[1] was born in 1729. He lived during the same time period as John Wesley, and he was called "The Terrific Fletcher." He pursued God with terrific passion, and he had an all-consuming, unquenchable fire within him.

Fletcher spent many hours kneeling in prayer. After he went home to Heaven in 1785, it was discovered that there was actually a spot on the floorboards in his home that was worn down from him spending many hours kneeling in prayer and pouring out his heart before the Lord. The wall in the same room, where he had waited and worshiped God in love and adoration, was stained by his breath.

After reading about the passion John Fletcher had for Jesus, I wept and wept. This made me hungrier for Him even more. I said, "O God, is there any stain or residue of my spending time with you?" One day as I was walking into my prayer room, I saw the stain on the wall where I always sat leaning against the wall. In my brokenness, I said, "Thank You, Lord, for opening my eyes and showing me the stain." I realized the Lord remembers and marks the very place where I spend time with Him.

Are you lovesick for Jesus?

Is He the craving of your heart?

How desperate are you to know Him?

He is calling you to come away with Him into His cloud-filled chamber.

PLEASE PRAY THIS WITH ME

O God of my life, I'm lovesick for you in this weary wilderness.
I thirst with the deepest longings to love you more,
with cravings in my heart that can't be described.
Such yearning grips my soul for you, my God!
I'm energized every time I enter
your heavenly sanctuary to seek more of your power
and drink in more of your glory.
For your tender mercies mean more to me than life itself.
How I love and praise you, God!
Daily I will worship you passionately and with all my heart.
My arms will wave to you like banners of praise.
I overflow with praise when I come before you,
for the anointing of your presence satisfies me like nothing else.
You are such a rich banquet of pleasure to my soul.
Psalm 63:1-5 (TPT)

May you fulfill your destiny as you passionately pursue Jesus with all your heart!

***Yong Brierly**, Lead Pastor and Revivalist*
River of Destiny Church
Lostant, Illinois

Note
1. TOZER, A.W., *My Daily Pursuit; Devotions For Every Day,* Regal, 2013, 24.

Part 2

Walking In Faith, Not By Sight

DAY 20

ENJOYING INTIMACY WITH OUR LORD

...the Lord used to speak to Moses face to face, just as a man speaks to his friend. **Exodus 33:11 (NKJV)**

In this critical hour, we must have direction and understanding from the Word and the Spirit. There needs to be a contending for a strong devotional life to our Lord. There is empowerment and anointing for those who surrender their self-life. A further preparation by and for the Lord must be our quest.

The Lord shares His desire for intimacy with His people by the analogy of the bride and bridegroom. He is preparing the bride with understanding, power, and beauty for the Kingdom of Glory. The broken, the lost, and the desperate will see the Glory of God through the bride, prepared as overcomers.

I urge you to prepare, come boldly before the throne of grace, and see the Lord high and lifted up. God will activate you to overcome the evil of the present and participate in the harvest of souls.

We read of and know men and women who obviously enjoy intimacy with Jesus. They are those who take time to cultivate and respond to the Lord's presence. There is a godly, submitted, and cooperative relationship in their lifestyle.

Remember, we too can seek a deeper intimacy with the Lord by setting aside the agenda of this hectic society. We must turn aside from lesser things and focus our attention on His voice and presence. Keep the First Commandment first!

The Lord appreciated being appreciated. The Lord desires to be wanted. He has much to share with those who appreciate and spend time set aside with Him. May we develop a greater sensitivity to His presence and turn aside from our routine when He beckons.

> ***Then Moses said, "I will now turn aside and see this great sight, why the bush does not burn."***
> **Exodus 3:3 (NKJV)**

> ***Thus the Lord used to speak to Moses face to face, just as a man speaks to his friend.*** **Exodus 33:11 (NKJV)**

What could be more intimate? Is there a parallel to that in our experience?

Intimacy with Jesus is a price worth sacrificing lesser things to attain. May we have that deep desire….

A place on Jesus' breast is awaiting you.

Reverend Jay T. Francis*, Founder and Pastor*
Rock Road Chapel Ministries and International Accelerated Missions
Berne, New York

Day 21

Math Lessons for Life

And let us not grow weary while doing good, for in due season we shall reap if we do not lose heart.
Galatians 6:9 (NKJV)

Algebra is a part of my life again. It's been nearly twenty years since I took algebra in high school, yet Monday through Friday my days are filled with algebraic symbols, functions, and those dreaded quadratic equations. As much as I loathe teaching my homeschooled children algebra, I have to marvel at the incredible journey that we have accomplished together, that brought us to the place where we are now conquering algebra.

When we first started homeschooling, my kids thought that they knew everything, and they didn't need me to teach them anything. They vaguely understood how numbers worked, and they thought that math was a breeze. In their minds, they were ready to tackle any math problem that existed. I can just imagine how their eyes would have popped out of their heads if I had placed the algebra book in front of them back then. They would have been completely unable to solve even the easiest problem in the algebra book at their age and understanding.

If I had tried to rush the process and teach algebra before my kids were ready, it would have been a complete train wreck. Looking back, I see how each lesson, each year, laid the foundation necessary to prepare us all to tackle the kinds of problems that we are faced with each day. Those years could not have been rushed. There is nothing that I could have done to make the learning process go faster. The necessary skills must be built over time. There are steps that simply cannot be skipped.

I'm reminded of the 400 years of waiting that took place between the books of Malachi and Matthew. I can only imagine how hard it was for the children of Israel to wait for their promised Messiah all those years. Talk about a long period of preparation! Yet God, in His infinite wisdom, knew just the right time to send His Son into the world. If He had come too early, the world would not have been prepared to spread the good news of the Gospel and carry the message far and wide! If the Greeks had not conquered the known world first, with their desire to "make the whole world Greece," they would not have compelled everyone to speak one common language, Greek. If the Romans hadn't been the next to try to conquer the world, they would not have built their elaborate system of roads that made travel quick and easy! God sent His Son at just the right time, when the gospel could be rapidly spread by His disciples in a common language, along safe and well-traveled routes.

Many of the plans that God has for you and me cannot be rushed. There is literally nothing that you can do to speed up His process sometimes. How hard it is to be patient and trust God's timing! But we know that God is meticulous in His process, and we can trust Him. However, there are some things that we can do to slow down His plans for us! We aren't exactly bystanders in this process! We have a lot of responsibility when it comes to seeing God's plans come to pass in our own lives.

If we want to be successful in anything, just like in algebra, we must be diligent and complete the foundational work that's assigned to us. One of the ways that you and I can slow down God's plan for our lives is through procrastination! Have you completed the last task that God gave you? Are you being diligent to complete the assignment that you were given, or have you become distracted along the way?

If my kids had let all their other subjects and activities take up too much of their time, and had constantly avoided their daily math lessons, they would never have made it to algebra. Busyness can be another reason we can't seem to move forward with our calling. Some of us are too busy doing a million things that we were never called to do, and it's getting in the way of getting on with our true calling! Is there something that's taking up all your time that you know is not part of God's plan for you?

A sure way to never fulfill the call of God on your life is to be disobedient. If one of my kids had dug their heels in and flat out refused to do math and algebra, possibly, college would not be in their future. If I am not obedient to do the things that I know for sure that God has asked of me, then I can be sure that He will not be giving me my next assignment any time soon.

If my children had been influenced by friends who hate math, they might have started to hate math too, to avoid being teased. Their progress in math would have slowed right down. If we keep our passion and our devotion a secret, and we act differently depending on who we are with, then we are letting the fear of man get in the way of our true calling. You're either all in or you're not. God is looking for people who are all in to accomplish His Kingdom plans on the earth.

A final way we can slow down our own progress is by becoming disconnected from the source. Those daily math lessons built a strong foundation that led to greater comprehension and knowledge! Your daily time in the "secret place" simply cannot be neglected if you want to move ahead with God's will for your life! Neglecting your time with God is sure to slow down His plans for you.

I may not be able to speed up God's plans for my life, but I don't want to slow them down either! Being obedient in the small things, spending time with Him daily, avoiding distractions, and looking at God alone for approval are some of the things that each of us can do while we wait on His timing for the rest to come to pass. Today, let's determine to get rid of all delays and distractions!

Heather Bartos, *Homeschool Mom and Worship Leader*
Cooperstown Assembly of God
Cooperstown, New York

Day 22

What Shall I Do?

So Moses cried out to the LORD, saying, "What shall I do with this people? They are almost ready to stone me!"
Exodus 17:4 (NKJV)

There is a moment in the life of every believer when we have to decide for ourselves what we choose to believe, what we will do about it, and why we choose to believe it. It's most often a moment of crisis when we have done the will of God and served Him with everything that is within us, yet things did not turn out the way we thought they would. We entered into our service to the Lord with a good heart and honest intentions, but the outcome was far from what we expected. Have you been there? If not, you will be some day.

For some, it could be how their children turned out after they spent their growing years trying to bring them into a relationship with God. For others, it might be the kind of employment they ended up with or the marriage relationship they found themselves in. No matter how hard they tried, things just went the wrong way. For each of us, it will be something different, but the end results are still the same.

We obeyed God and believed that everything would turn out right, only to discover we are in the opposite circumstance than we trusted Him for. This is the moment of crises that the devil often takes advantage of. Our faith is shaken, our heart is struggling, our emotions are raw, and we begin to second guess what caused the problem in the first place. Without knowing it, we can begin to doubt ourselves and the decisions we made that got us there. Unless this gets fully resolved, we can even begin to doubt God.

This is the very place Moses found himself, in Exodus 17:4. He had worked amazing miracles with God and delivered the children of Israel from 430 years of bondage and slavery. He had parted the Red Sea, which then was restored and destroyed the Egyptian army. He had even made bitter water sweet so everyone could drink. He had cried out to God and seen bread fall down out of Heaven. Yet, after all this, the people were still grumbling; and they were ready to stone him to death. All this happened because they were once again thirsty and wanted water. They were not grateful, appreciative, or filled with joy for all that had already been provided. Oh no! They were just the opposite, and Moses had reached his breaking point.

We read the following in Exodus 17:4: "So Moses cried out to the LORD, saying, 'What shall I do to this people? A little more and they will stone me'." Earlier in the book of Exodus, we read about the struggle Moses had with God when he encountered Him in the backside of the wilderness. God called him to go to Egypt, and Moses had no desire to go back to the place he had escaped from 40 years earlier. In fact, he told God, "I don't speak well so please send somebody else." Because of this, God selected the brother of Moses, Aaron, to go with him. Then, Moses had another moment of crisis, but that time it wasn't with God, it's was with God's people.

If you belong to the Lord, and are part of a local church, that moment of crisis is going to happen to you. Every local church is filled with broken souls. They may love God, but that does not change the internal struggles and the pain the world has inflicted on them, that they still need to face. The church is not a perfect place, and the people in it are far from perfect. They are going to disappoint you. They may even be the cause of your moment of crisis and pain, when you ask, "What shall I do?" When that happens, and it will happen eventually, you are going to have to make a decision. Will you believe God and trust Him, or will you believe the circumstance that surrounds you and run?

If you're going to be truly successful in your walk with God, that defining moment of crisis is so very important. In fact, it will actually determine the rest of your life and the depth of your Christian faith.

Cling to the Lord, and believe He is bigger than the pain you're feeling. He will become the source of your strength. The other alternative is that you cling to the pain and the offense. If you do, from that moment on, it will be the controlling force of your life. The decision you make in your moment of crisis, when you ask the question, "What shall I do?" is the most important decision you will ever make. It will define your walk; it will shape your faith; it will determine your future.

Consider this: Are you willing to sacrifice all God intends to do with you, by holding on to that which can only do you harm? When you are hurting and ask the question, "What shall I do?" wait for God to give you the answer after you have bathed it in prayer and settled your emotions. From that posture of rest, you will hear His voice and always make the right choice. Let the peace of God that guards your heart and mind in Christ Jesus show you the way!

William Emmons, *Prophet, Pastor, and Author of Prophets & Prophecy*
Prophetic Destiny Ministries and Life Christian Center Church
Johnstown, New York

Day 23

Overcoming Faith

For whatsoever is born of God overcometh the world: and this is the victory that overcometh the world, even our faith. **1 John 5:4 (KJV)**

There are obstacles that stand in our way that can keep us from miracles and victory. It takes faith to overcome these obstacles. The Bible gives many examples how we too can overcome and have victory.

One of my favorites is the object lesson Jesus gave when he healed the daughter of the woman from Canaan. Here is the account from Matthew Chapter 15, verses 21 thru 28 (KJV):

Then Jesus went thence, and departed into the coasts of Tyre and Sidon.

And, behold, a woman of Canaan came out of the same coasts, and cried unto him, saying, "Have mercy on me, O Lord, thou son of David; my daughter is grievously vexed with a devil."

But he answered her not a word. And his disciples came and besought him, saying, "Send her away; for she crieth after us."

But he answered and said, "I am not sent but unto the lost sheep of the house of Israel."

Then came she and worshipped him, saying, "Lord, help me."

But he answered and said, "It is not meet to take the children's bread, and to cast it to dogs."

And she said, "Truth, Lord: yet the dogs eat of the crumbs which fall from their masters' table."

Then Jesus answered and said unto her, "O woman, great is thy faith: be it unto thee even as thou wilt. And her daughter was made whole from that very hour."

When you first read this passage, you get the impression that Jesus did not care about this woman or her problem. It looks like He did not want to help her; however, we know the true heart of Jesus. He cared deeply and wanted to help her, but He also knew she was a woman of "great faith." Jesus is using this account to teach us what "overcoming faith" looks like and how we too can overcome and obtain miracles.

Listed here in this account are the obstacles you will face when you need a miracle and how you can overcome them like the woman from Canaan did.

OBSTACLE NUMBER 1:
NO ANSWER FROM GOD

"Have mercy on me, O Lord, thou son of David; my daughter is grievously vexed with a devil." But he answered her not a word.

How often have you prayed and asked God for something, but the heavens seemed like brass? No answer.... It seems like God does not care about you or your problem. But "overcoming faith" knows that God does care! There must be a reason why there is no answer. Remember Daniel? For 21 days there was no answer to his prayers, but come to find out, Daniel was heard the first time he prayed; and an angel was sent immediately with the answer, but an evil spirit had fought against the angel. There are reasons why you are not getting the answer, but if you have "overcoming faith," you will realize it is not God that is holding anything back from you.

What is the right response to obstacle Number 1? The woman from Canaan showed us with her great faith: "And his disciples came and besought him, saying, Send her away; for she crieth after us." Her response was not to give up and think *God isn't answering. I guess it is His will for me to suffer,* but she got ahold of his disciples and besought them. The right response is to start calling on every man and woman of God you can and get them to go to the Lord on your behalf!

OBSTACLE NUMBER 2: THE MIRACLE IS NOT FOR YOU

But he answered and said, "I am not sent but unto the lost sheep of the house of Israel."

How often have you heard about someone else getting their miracle, but it wasn't you? You believe God can do miracles. You have seen others get theirs. You read in the Bible where Jesus healed everybody who came to Him, but you are not getting yours. Soon a voice begins to speak to you, *It's not for you. God did it for others, but He won't help you. Jesus was sent to help people... but not you.* Again, Jesus is using this Canaan woman to teach us how to overcome by faith.

What was her reaction when Jesus in effect said miracles were not for her? "Then came she and worshipped him, saying, Lord, help me." Keep worshipping Jesus. Keep trusting in who He is. Know that He does want to help you.... In fact, He died to help you. Stand fast in who He is and what He did for you. Worship Him for it. Personalize and make it your own… saying, "Lord, help me. You did for others… now help ME."

OBSTACLE NUMBER 3:
YOU ARE NOT WORTHY TO GET A MIRACLE

"It is not meet to take the children's bread, and to cast it to dogs."

By this, Jesus is showing us the last and greatest obstacle that you must overcome to obtain your miracle: That you are not good enough… you are not worthy. You are just a dog… not one of God's children.

What was the response to this by the woman of Canaan… this woman of great "overcoming faith"? "And she said, 'Truth, Lord: yet the dogs eat of the crumbs which fall from their masters' table'." Yes Lord, I am not worthy. After all, who is worthy? All have sinned and come short of the Glory of God. But I know you love and provide even for dogs. Let some crumbs fall from your hand, and I will be made whole.

IN SUMMARY

"Overcoming faith" trusts in the fact that God loves you and wants to help you… in spite of the circumstances and in the face of negatives and opposition. If you ever doubt God's desire to help you, just gaze at the cross. You will see every fiber of His being, striving to offer up the sacrifice that paid for your miracle.

Reverend Mark A. Swiger, BTh., DDiv.; *Evangelist and Author of Miracles and Multitudes and What Is a Disciple and How Do You Make One?*
Crossville, Tennessee

IN CLOSING

I pray that this book has both encouraged and challenged you to trust in God in greater measure than you ever have before. He is always faithful to His Word, and He can not lie.

God knows you; He loves you; He created you with specific plans and purposes for your life. Just as He did supernatural things in the Glory Stories that you read about here, He wants to give you your own Glory Stories.

I believe that we are entering into a time of great revival and awakening, where we will see more healings, deliverances, miracles, supernatural answers to prayer, and angelic visitations. Please be open to all that God has for you during this season.

May God bless you; prepare you; strengthen you; lead you; guide you; and give you wisdom, knowledge, and understanding as you walk with Him. This is an exciting time to be alive! After all, you were created for SUCH A TIME AS THIS!

Salvation Prayer

Maybe you picked this book up to read it just out of curiosity. If so, I don't believe that it was by accident or chance but by divine destiny.

God desires that you not only know about Him but that you would come into a real, vibrant, living, relationship with Him. If you don't already know Jesus as your Lord and Savior and you want to, please pray the following prayer from deep within your heart to enter into a relationship with Him. As you begin your walk of faith, He WILL begin to reveal Himself to you.

Dear Jesus,

I admit that I'm a sinner, and I need You. Thank you for dying on the cross in my place and taking my punishment. Please forgive me for my sins and come into my heart and be my Savior and my Lord. Please help me to live for You from this day forward. Thank you for making me part of Your family. In Jesus' Name, Amen.

If you prayed this prayer sincerely from your heart, you are now a child of God! You have just taken your first step in your journey with Him. Welcome to His family!!!

ACKNOWLEDGMENTS

PROOFREADERS

A huge "Thank You" to both **Barbara Griffin** and **Cheryl Merriman** for proofreading this book. Your attention to detail was greatly appreciated.

Made in the USA
Middletown, DE
18 May 2021

39190469R00073